The
Risk
Factor

Also by Deborah Perry Piscione and available
from Palgrave Macmillan Trade

Secrets of Silicon Valley:
What Everyone Else Can Learn from
the Innovation Capital of the World

The
Risk
Factor

WHY EVERY ORGANIZATION
NEEDS BIG BETS, BOLD CHARACTERS,
AND THE OCCASIONAL
SPECTACULAR FAILURE

Deborah Perry Piscione

palgrave
macmillan

First published in 2014 by PALGRAVE MACMILLAN® TRADE
in the United States—a division of St. Martin's Press LLC, 175 Fifth
Avenue, New York, NY 10010.

Palgrave® and Macmillan® are registered trademarks in the United
States, the United Kingdom, Europe and other countries.

ISBN: 978-1-137-27928-6

Library of Congress Cataloging-in-Publication Data

Piscione, Deborah Perry.
   The risk factor : why every organization needs big bets, bold
characters, and the occasional spectacular failure / Deborah Perry
Piscione.
  pages   cm
   ISBN 978-1-137-27928-6 (hardback)
   1. Risk. 2. Strategic planning. 3. Value. 4. Success in business.
I. Title.
HB615.P487 2014
658.15'5—dc23

                                                           2014016535

A catalogue record of the book is available from the British Library.

Design by Letra Libre

First edition: December 2014

10 9 8 7 6 5 4 3 2 1

Printed in the United States of America.

Contents

PART I

Introduction

The only man who never makes mistakes is the man who never does anything.

—Theodore Roosevelt

We are all born risk-takers. It's this innate drive that has allowed the human race to come so far. But the lifelong process of socialization has a way of tamping down those daring impulses. Little by little, we are told what to do, how to do it, what not to do, where to go, where not to go, and so on, and pretty soon most of us forget how to go out on a limb. But a very few maintain their boldness, an ability to challenge the norms and to fight for better ways for us to live and work in the world. They don't dwell on their life's unknowns. These are the people who have found their relevance and who, until their last breath, will be figuring out how to go beyond the edge of the limb.

In my last book, Secrets of Silicon Valley: What Everyone Else Can Learn from the Innovation Capital of the World, *like any writer, I wrestled with the depth of my conclusions. I recognized that, in the end, I had only scratched the surface of why Silicon Valley was such an alluring anomaly. Yes, the Valley is a meritocracy that rewards value irrespective of age, experience, gender, skin color, or dialect. Many of its companies continue to raise the bar for organizational competence in the twenty-first century, and they not only lead their respective industries—they're reinventing our economy. Yet the most anomalous characteristic of this innovative region, in my opinion, is that it's not really a geographic location at all but a mind-set. Its chief principles are openness, trust, collaboration— and, most important, a willingness to take risks, at all costs. No idea is crazy—in fact, sometimes the more out there you are, the more respect you garner from your peers. (Witness serial entrepreneur Elon Musk's vow to build a high-speed train that travels faster than the speed of sound.)[1] A failed company or idea isn't a black mark on your resume in Silicon Valley—more often it's a badge of honor, a sign that you just need to wait for a better time, a better* place, a better team. Silicon Valley contains the most entrepreneurial mind-set on Earth, is on the edge of nearly all disruptions, and inspires a like-minded spirit to debunk all things traditional. In such environments, process doesn't drive creativity; rather, the reverse—creativity and chaos first, process later. It is an infectious environment, full of helpful people who seem to know how to follow an undocumented set of rules on how things get done—a way of doing things that is found nowhere else on the planet.

In 2006, I moved to Silicon Valley and never looked back. Why? Because I went from being deeply indoctrinated in the most bureaucratic and hierarchical culture to unlearning toxicity and embracing a pervasive sense of optimism that anything, *anything* is possible. I began my career in the gridlock of Washington, DC, spending 18 years there, first as a legislative aide in the U.S. Congress and the White House and, later on, as a media commentator for MSNBC, FOX News, and CNN—environments that define the rules for how to play on people's fears. You learn how to play the game and to be careful on your way up; truly, you never know who you will meet on your way down. If you don't learn the rules, you get eaten alive. If you try to offer leadership, members within your own political party will first ask why you are doing that and then ask you to quietly stand in rank and file . . . *or else*. I have so many stories.

After I moved to Silicon Valley, I began to recognize that people are innately collaborative, trusting, supportive, and fearless. Because of this unique ecosystem, I was able to build out three companies in six years: BettyConfidential, Alley to the Valley, and ChumpGenius. When my cofounder and I messed up a viable offer to sell BettyConfidential early on, our investor stood by our side and never made us feel like failures. She just expected us to figure it out and work toward a solution. It took us four more years to see serious acquisition activity.

Throughout the writing of both books, I had incredible access to some of the world's greatest innovators (mostly West Coast–based chief executive, chief technology, and chief information officers, in addition to venture capitalists, lawyers, and intellectual property experts), and what amazed me the most was that these people felt that they had just as much to learn from me as I did from them. Often I would be asking questions, and their follow-up was "I'd like your opinion on . . ." It wasn't that I had all the answers, but they wanted to learn from what I was seeing, what I was hearing. This just would not happen in Washington, where people's favorite pastime is one-sided pontification of my way or the highway.

This is a book about risk's perplexities, its opportunities, its perils, and for most people, our collective fear of it. Risk applies to every aspect of the human condition and is a product of both nature and nurture. Yet the lingering questions are: Can the desire to take risk be learned? What factors are necessary to create a risk-taking and innovative environment? And most important, how do you become the person who takes the right risks at the most critical time?

Our companies and communities are largely designed to mitigate risk, so it is no surprise that we celebrate, even idolize, those leaders who looked risk in the eye and came out on top. The subjects of my research are an audacious group. They are individuals who are changing the world, the way we think, the way we do business, the way we live our lives. They have risked their educations, their careers, their financial well-being, their families, and their reputations just so they can contribute to the greater good. And they all have the battle scars and setbacks to prove it. These people are the bold characters who make the big bets.

Some of these great minds are no longer with us, and there is no guarantee that the organizations mentioned in this book will be here in 5 years, much less 50 years from now. Tellingly, several of the efforts described in this book were considered failures at the time, although we now know that the world or their respective organizations just weren't ready for them yet. Accordingly, this book is focused primarily on risk as a leadership tool in business, but with the understanding that it is individuals who drive these efforts.

It is hard to fail, but it is worse never to have tried to succeed.

—Theodore Roosevelt

At the turn of the twentieth century, America was riding a wave of euphoric optimism, mostly due to a surge of technological advancements. It was known as the Gilded Age. Railroads were expanding, automobiles were getting more powerful, and the Wright brothers launched the first flight. People were exploring the Arctic and expanding westward. It was also a long-awaited period of extraordinary economic growth that came on the heels of multiple banking crises. The Panic of 1893 was the worst economic depression the young United States had ever experienced, due to railroad overbuilding and shaky financing backed by the gold supply. Many banks closed their doors, there was a run on currency, and businesses and manufacturers were not able to operate because they had no cash to buy materials or pay employees. The panic led to the collapse of some Wall Street brokerage houses and the failure of national, state, and private savings banks and mortgage institutions. The era had many of the characteristics that we are experiencing on the heels of the financial crisis of 2008.

The reason I raise this slice of economic history is that the United States and the world will naturally continue to be in a state of economic and/or financial perplexity, frequently in the mode of economic downturn or recovery. The very nature of economics is that no economy is meant to be stable for long. First, investors make money off economic instability; they make money when markets go up and down and reject the very nature of stability. Second, there are natural highs and lows of economic cycles, natural states of unemployment, and new versions of crony capitalism are perpetually brewing, as some Wall Street crook will be tempted to profit from some ambiguity at the expense of confused and susceptible consumers. The point is that we have to persevere no matter how broken or beaten down we feel. Tough economic times expose good leaders and bad leaders, and the good ones understand that volatility presents an opportunity to take risks—because good leaders realize that there is risk in not being in the game.

The turn of the twentieth century gave us some of our most adventurous heroes in business, politics, exploration, and science, men and women who made the world what it is today—people such as Alexander Graham Bell, the Wright brothers, William Jennings Bryan, Andrew Carnegie, Amelia Earhart, Thomas Edison, Henry Ford, William Randolph Hearst, William Henson, Charles Evans Hughes, John Pierpont Morgan, Ransom Eli Olds, Admiral Robert Peary, John D. Rockefeller, Theodore Roosevelt, Leland Sanford, Nikola Tesla, Cornelius Vanderbilt, and Woodrow Wilson.

Among the risk-takers who reshaped society at the turn of the century was Theodore Roosevelt. On September 14, 1901, he was sworn in as the twenty-sixth president of the United States at the age of 42. At the time, he was one year younger than President John Kennedy when he was sworn in, and he's still the youngest serving president in American history. Roosevelt ascended to the presidency after the assassination of President William McKinley Jr. Then in 1904 he won the presidency with the largest percentage of the popular vote (56.4 percent) since the uncontested vote of 1820. Roosevelt was committed to breaking up monopolies on the home front and imperialism abroad. He was also the force behind the Panama Canal, a key conduit for maritime trade that fostered economic advantages for the United States and other trading nations.

His slogan "Speak softly and carry a big stick" reminded his foes that he could negotiate gently but was not afraid to use military force when necessary. Roosevelt's realpolitik nonmilitary strategy helped to end the Russo-Japanese war, and for that, he is one of three sitting presidents who has received the Nobel Peace Prize.

The country embraced his leadership as head of the Republican Party and the Progressive movement as well as his persona as naturalist, explorer, author, and soldier. He lobbied for high tariffs, the gold standard, and antitrust policies, even over his party's objections. Roosevelt set bold, audacious goals and, as a result, inspired people to think about things in a new way and attempt the seemingly impossible. When Teddy Roosevelt was president, it was our politicians who gave others the inspiration to achieve greatness.

WHERE'S OUR NEXT SPACE RACE?

On May 25, 1961, President John F. Kennedy announced, before a special joint session of Congress, one of the most daring goals in history: to send a man to the moon. The decision was prompted partly by fear that the Soviets, who had launched the first satellite, Sputnik, into orbit in 1957, were winning the so-called space race. Moreover, on April 12, 1961, Soviet cosmonaut Yuri Gagarin was the first human to be launched into space in a rocket-propelled satellite. On May 5, U.S. astronaut Alan Shepard flew into space on the *Mercury* spacecraft, a suborbital flight that lasted all of 15 minutes and reached a peak altitude of 116 miles. Gagarin, in comparison, had orbited Earth in a total flight time of 108 minutes.[2]

Not all Americans wanted to send a man to the moon, but most wanted to make it clear that the nation stood for something. As in the Gilded Age, the transcendent wonder of technology abounded in the 1960s. Where could space travel lead us in the future? What would our world look like in 1984 and beyond? Was it to be George Orwell's view, or more of a *Gulliver's Travels* meets *Star Trek*? Kennedy's proposal offered enormous potential rewards not only to the science, medical, and technology communities but also to society as a whole. He made the Baby Boomer generation believe that our nation could ascend to heights above our world—that anything is possible.

Now fast-forward to the beginning of the twenty-first century, and I ask: Where is our next space race? It will not come from government. Why? We have witnessed the massive rise of the global economy and growth of Third World consumerism. We have been stirred by a tumultuous mix of distrust of our governments coupled with a deep concern about both politically motivated terrorism and random acts of terrorism.

The United States is no longer the world's sole superpower. China is racing to rival Europe and America on every front, and the BRIC (Brazil, Russia, India, China) countries, which are all deemed to be at a similar stage of newly advanced economic development, are growing rapidly into geopolitical power players. These countries have made bold bets in their quest to rise to world powers and elevate the fortunes of their citizens. We are only beginning to bear witness to the strength of what these economies are and what they have the potential to become.

And during this time, citizens of the United States have, for the most part, elected risk-averse leaders, powerful men and women who rule more by poll numbers and political contributions and less by a desire for great forward leaps. Today our political leaders won't make a move without polling their most important constituents, and corporate leaders follow the wishes of their biggest stakeholders, favoring safe incremental improvements over bold, game-changing strategies that could redefine the future. The result is a static political and business culture that generates forgettable results—even as the world demands big solutions.

"Inertia is the most powerful physical force in politics," says Kellyanne Conway, president and CEO of The Polling Company and Woman Trend and a 25-year veteran of polling. "Unless and until overtaken by friction, things at rest tend to stay at rest. Most politicians are allergic to risk, preferring to play it safe, within the two 40-yard lines, lest they anger core constituencies. Politicians fear that taking a risk on the job will lead to actually risking their jobs."[3]

Politics and government tend to punish risk and thwart entrepreneurial thinking. "In Washington, playing it safe keeps you popular and employed. In real life, it makes you predictable and stagnant. In recent years, many business leaders are behaving more like politicians. Drunk with polls of consumers or constituents, doing what they can to keep voters and shareholders happy, leaders in both business and politics have significant skin in the status quo, with less incentive toward innovation," Conway continues.

America has seen remarkable gains in business over the past decade, but most of these gains have been driven by rapid advancements in information technologies and biosciences. The digital revolution has disrupted entire industries. The completion of the Human Genome Project marked a new age of life sciences, giving hope for cures for cancer and aging. Yet other examples of audacious advancements in business and society are harder to find.

Why?

Thrown into the mix is the increased power of private enterprise, a combination of both financial prowess and crony capitalism, all having a crippling impact on American workers. Did the dot-com/Enron/WorldCom collapses skin our knees too deeply? Did 9/11 heighten our fears to an unimaginable place? Did the Great Recession of 2008 drive us past our economic breaking point? Have gnawing fear and continuing unscrupulous business practices ceded our future greatness to bold leaders elsewhere in the world? Have we been so beaten down that we are experiencing paralysis?

Where is the modern-day Teddy? The one who notably said that it is better to try and fail than never to try at all. I first saw this quote on Theodore Roosevelt Island in Washington, DC, in the fall of 1988, and it became my guiding mantra for my life. Every Sunday morning, irrespective of the weather, I jumped on my bike and rode to the island to remind myself why I took the huge risk of moving to Washington not knowing a soul or having any connections to viable jobs. A few months later, two men I met took a chance on me and helped me get my first job on Capitol Hill with U.S. Senator Connie Mack. For their support, I remain grateful.

What makes a country great is not its absolute levels of wealth or growth but its willingness to overcome adversity, economic hardship, and civil injustice and to engage in experiment. By embracing risk, new ideas are explored, learning is ignited, passions are fueled, and forward-thinking leaders emerge. Conversely, by mitigating risk, a country turns on itself, fighting about the present rather than planning for the future. We see it in today's political leadership, where bold new policy ideas are ridiculed as "job killers," "subsidies for the rich," or, most damning of all, "un-American." The ripple effects spread throughout the world, because, still, when America sneezes, the rest of the world catches a cold.

We need to get out of this fishbowl and find our next space race. Doing so will take different kinds of leaders in politics and organizations—not leaders with the leadership skills to recognize just what is, but those who comprehend what can be. Leaders who think less about short-term profitability and political expediency and instead thrive on embracing long-term value creation. Those who think boldly about political, social, and economic issues across the board. In this century, as government becomes less and less relevant in our lives, and bold risk-takers and their entrepreneurial prowess become our modern-day heroes, our next space race could come from anyone, at any time, and from anywhere.

THE TAXONOMY OF RISK

Risk remains an undefined leadership tool, yet it is the most vital apparatus of our time. Without risk, there can be no reward. Yet, even today, the incumbent business world is steeped in traditional, hierarchical practices that not only preclude it from moving forward but also kill its relevance and perhaps its existence. For this book, I interviewed too many executives who complained about their backward-thinking boards of directors and the seeming impossibility of cultural change within their organizations. I spoke to countless middle managers who felt beaten down—unappreciated for their contributions—and frequently commented that their organizations suck the life out of them.

The great irony is that there is no better time for risk than right now. Technology allows us to experiment at little to no cost, and corporate profitability is at an all-time high. With the advances of technology, a small cadre of people can create an entrepreneurial venture that only governments and large corporations could have started a generation ago. An entrepreneur type can remain at a large organization and have the financial resources to make the big bets. Imagine the possibilities.

I consult and speak to large corporations about Silicon Valley's unique risk-taking culture, and the one question that consistently comes up is: How should I see risk? As an answer, I ask leaders to picture in their minds a large and majestic oak tree in the heat of a warm summer day. At first you just see the tree, casting its solid shadow on the ground below. But on closer examination, if you open up your imagination, you can start to notice how a tree might exemplify almost any organization. The trunk of the tree is the cultural foundation of the organization. The branches extending from the trunk represent the lines of business, such as products and services. The thinner branches that grow out of the extend-ing branches symbolize the potential extent of the organization's growth, in as many directions as there is space.

Look even closer and you will have a revelation: Most of the space occupied by this tree is actually the air between its branches and leaves. You then realize that the space around the tree dictates the tree's shape and its room for future growth. That space also determines the success of dropped seeds in the surrounding fertile ground of new clients and customers. I call these the open spaces. Opportunity lies in the open spaces and is fed by the roots bur-rowed into the bountiful soil of loyal clients and consumers. Risk can be seen as navigating the open spaces. The farther you reach, the more likely it is that the branch will snap and you will fall to the ground. Yet that is also where the greatest opportunity lies, as few have the courage to reach that far.

Most of us have had that moment. We're about to step up to the podium, jump off a 500-foot cliff, ask someone to marry us, or give the okay on a multimillion-dollar investment. Our palms are sweaty, our heartbeat increases, and perhaps we obsess over whether we are doing the right thing. We have positioned ourselves to go out on a limb.

This book is for those who yearn to drop new seeds and for those who crave exploration of their organization's open spaces. It is for those who wish to "zag" when conventional wisdom says "zig." It is for those who want to stand up for what is right, even if the personal and professional cost is seemingly devastating. It is for those who are looking for their inner Teddy, who wish to blaze a new path, redefine the rules, and even change the world for the greater good. This book is for those seeking their relevance.

CHAPTER ONE

Why Risk-Taking Isn't Gambling

*What Poker, Jazz, and the Toyota Assembly
Line Can Teach You about Business*

If you've ever seen the World Series of Poker on television, the most notable characteristic is the potpourri of humanity: Sitting around a circular table are players with shirts and hats stamped with the logos of online gaming sites, young men cocooned in oversize hoodies, not-so-young men wearing sunglasses indoors with headphones plugged into their ears, and the occasional enigmatic woman. Their chip stacks vary in size and color; several players shuffle, roll, and otherwise fondle their chips with seasoned dexterity. In the middle of the table are five cards faceup, and a few players have two cards facedown in front of them. You can see that the tension is high, with one player raising the bet, applying pressure to his opponents. The next player folds after some contemplation, leaving only one other player to bet or fold. He stares at the player who raised the stakes, looking for some small tell that will betray the competitor's confidence in his hand. After some silent, internal dialogue, the player raises, tripling the bet of the player who first raised. On your TV screen, you can see what the hidden cards are. You know who has the weakest hand. All the first player needs to do is call the hand and win a huge pot. You may find yourself talking to the TV screen, imploring him to call. Time ticks away as the tension builds. Finally the man folds, and the dealer pushes the massive pile of chips over to the player with the worst hand. Welcome to Texas Hold 'Em.[1]

Poker is a game of unknowns, luck, and percentages. Generally, the players vary as much as the cards. Some play by mathematical probabilities. Some play on momentum. Some play by observing behavioral patterns or microgestures that serve as tells. And some play by pure instinct. The perfect hand comes along rarely, so aggressive risk-taking is a key part of the game. Yet, in the blink of a bleary eye, hours of careful calculation can be wiped out by a bold gamble.

LESSONS FROM GAMBLING THAT CAN OR CANNOT BE APPLIED TO RISK-TAKING

The classic risk question is this: Where is the line between a calculated risk and a reckless gamble? Can you win big or lose big either way? The answer is "yes, *but . . .*" Calculated risk requires tools, skills, and knowledge that are, in one or more ways, left out of the gambler's equation. So, what can we learn from gamblers about enabling and mitigating risk?

- **In poker, you must understand not only what you can gain but what you can lose.** Smart risk-takers learn how to quickly calculate their gain/loss ratio and walk away when the math isn't in their favor. If you can't lose everything, then don't risk everything. Good poker players often measure the possible loss to their own chip stack versus the gain of the chips in the pot and assess the level of acceptable risk in continuing with their hand. You often hear players say something like, "I had a 3-to-1 payoff," meaning that for every chip they add to the pot, and potentially lose, they gain three back if they win. The higher the ratio, the more reasonable the risk.

- **Soak up as much contradictory knowledge as possible about anything related to the risk you are taking.** You should be seeking out opinions that clash with your own thoughts and feelings, no matter how uncomfortable doing so makes you, because it helps you see the full spectrum of possibilities, good and bad. Every action causes a reaction, and reckless gamblers rarely look past the first layer of consequences to understand the ripple effect their gamble may cause. The best poker players, by contrast, are expert observers, watching movements in other players' eyes, ears, and mouths for information about how other players bet. Smart players often bet in controlled amounts on hands they believe will lose, just to assess how other players act, so they can use that information later in the game.

- **Play what's dealt.** If you are dealt a pair of jacks as your hole cards and you fail to calculate all other possible hands that can be played, you might concentrate so much on the third jack that was just dealt on the river that you fail to notice that the same jack also completes a flush for another player. If you bet big, thinking that you have the best hand, you will lose your shirt. Good players will see the possibility of other hands that might beat their own and adjust their betting accordingly.

- **Learn how to chunk.** No two situations are alike; flexibility and adaptability are essential. David Epstein, in his book *The Sports Gene,* describes the concept of "chunking," which is the subconscious practice of segmenting information based on patterns you have witnessed before.[2] Epstein says that chess masters and elite athletes chunk information, recalling patterns that have worked well in the past. For example, a grandmaster chess player only needs to remember a few chunks of several chess pieces, rather than the whole board, because the relationships between the pieces have great meaning for the game. Epstein points out that we have a much easier time remembering a 20-word sentence than 20 random words with no meaningful relationship to one another. Those highly practiced at any activity naturally link multiple pieces of information into one thought process.

  A highly skilled Texas Hold 'Em player can chunk information—such as which community cards have been dealt, where players are sitting relative to the dealer and the big blind (when the two players to the left of the dealer are required to place compulsory bets before the cards are dealt), the types of bets each player makes on a given hand, the body language each exhibits, and dozens of other factors—to assess that singular moment. If, after all these things are considered, a player determines that a risky move will have a higher chance of succeeding, then he or she will pounce on the opportunity. That is what happened in the poker hand described earlier. The winning player read indicators that the other player's hand was good but not the best. The winner instantly exploited that weakness by betting at such a high level, and with such confidence, that the other player feared he had misread his chances of winning, and the cost of losing suddenly became too high to tolerate.

- **Embrace failure.** Separate your emotions about winning from the win itself. And when you lose, celebrate being a little smarter than you were five minutes ago. True gamblers, unlike rational risk-takers, tend to need the high of winning and confuse it with accomplishment. The term "on tilt" refers to players who have shed their discipline and gone reckless. Players on tilt rarely win in the long term.

FROM THE GAME OF POKER TO THE ELEMENTS OF RISK-TAKING

One of the reasons why risk has yet to be convincingly defined as an apparatus in the leadership toolbox is because it has been held hostage by finance departments and entirely undervalued as it applies to leadership and management. Business schools and management authorities have researched, written, and spoken exhaustively about how to create or improve on products and services to stay competitive. Risk-taking has never been highlighted as a key part of what makes great businesspeople and leaders tick, even by people or companies that excel at it naturally. And when something such as risk-taking is not exercised, just like a muscle in our body, it atrophies.

An organization can build a foundation of readiness for risk-taking, broken down into three action categories:

1. Improvisational risk
2. Operational risk
3. Game-changing risk

Improvisational Risk

Every time you engage in an unscripted activity, from a phone call with a customer, to a problem-solving meeting, to choosing a new restaurant for a client lunch, you are improvising.

You are taking a risk that can have a grave impact on your reputation. A significant portion of organizational advance and personal growth comes from these improvised moments, often responses to opportunities. The impact of these moments can be measured along a sliding scale that is bordered by no change (static) on one end and complete change (chaos) on the other. This is what I call the *risk continuum*.

RISK CONTINUUM

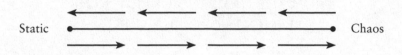

Every instance of improvised activity invites the opportunity to slide along the scale from static to chaos and back. The farther you slide toward chaos, the more chance you have of creating something new and amazing. Genius lives much closer to the chaos end of the risk continuum. But the closer you get toward chaos, shedding the safety of guidelines, rules, and structure, the higher your chances for failure. Safety and security generally are found toward the static end of the continuum. The farther we slide toward that safe end, the more we are willing to give up and the further we limit the promise of innovation and our ability to react to new or changing external forces.

These external forces, over which we have no control, are increasing in speed, strength, and complexity and are causing us to learn how to better negotiate the chaotic end of our behavior. The exponential pace in today's business climate propels the current struggle between change and tradition. How do you know, at any one time, how to improvise enough to create something great without tripping over the line into chaos?

The Improvisation of Jazz

Think about jazz. As an art form, jazz was developed to celebrate the moment by creating music in real time. It was a reaction to the more rigid, formal, and expensive genres that dominated the period, such as chamber ensembles and orchestras. Jazz brought together accomplished musicians who liked the social nature of a band and wanted to play music that both held to a framework and explored new ground. This process created a handy by-product: an incredibly advanced template for team-based communications that allows for maximum risk-taking.

Michael Gold, who teaches jazz theory to business leaders at the Kellogg School of Management at Northwestern University, says: "Jazz isn't about producing an object of art like a painting or a sculpture. Jazz is actually a social process that results in the constant creation of new ideas and innovative musical interaction." Gold describes a jazz ensemble as a high-performance team that practices a set of shared behaviors. He calls these behaviors "The Five Dynamics of Jazz":

1. **Autonomy.** True autonomy depends on the equity of each party concerned. Leadership is no longer a static position but one that is dependent on the ability to respond to changing needs and delegate to others based on their areas of expertise. In the jazz ensemble, the constant transition between leading and support strengthens and expands the capabilities of both the individual and the team.

2. **Passion.** Jazz is a culture in which passion and motivation are generated by a sense of authenticity. When we believe what we are doing is important and has a purpose larger than ourselves, we develop passion that energizes not just ourselves but also the people we work with. All too often, businesses attempt to instill passion through external triggers that tend to quash the spirit rather than kindle it. The passion of emotional commitment comes from within and is supported by a belief in the integrity of the organizational culture.

3. **Risk.** Progress is impossible without a willingness to take chances. Risk is not an option in jazz or for any company that wants to be solvent ten years from now. In jazz we mitigate the risk of change through creative destruction: extracting the

core values from successful past initiatives and using them to reinvent the idea in constantly changing contexts. . . . We're minimizing the structure. We simplify the score. We're taking only what's essential to coordinate us in time and intention. We're letting go of all of the other rules and protocols that keep us from responding to the unexpected in whatever way we need.

4. **Innovation.** Innovation is not a "what" but a "how." It is the result of fusing past knowledge and experience with an exploration of . . . new possibility. In jazz, innovation implies a creative partnership between the "leadership" of the soloist and the "support" of the rhythm section. The rhythm section provides a foundation of support for the exploration of the soloist. The discoveries of the soloist expand and strengthen that foundation in a continual cycle of innovative growth. It is a process that delivers both support and safety and rejects stasis and complacency.

5. **Listening.** Listening in the moment—suspending assumption and expectation—is critical for engaging the uncertainty of change. When we truly listen we allow ourselves to hear the dissonance and friction that new ideas can often generate. To listen in the moment means to listen empathically—to suspend assumptions and judgments that are rooted in our past experience so we can hear what we don't yet understand.[3]

You may not be a fan of jazz, but the face of modern music has been indelibly shaped by these principles. The farther away that we move from music as a recorded product toward music as live music performance, the more these principles apply. Can you imagine being a jazz artist and having to read a 56-page manual on what to do and what not to do? Jazz ensembles look for musicians not only with mastery of their instruments but also with proven improvisational skills. It is the live performance that yields memorable moments and acts of jaw-dropping genius. Every day we must negotiate undefined areas of our work and the open spaces in our lives. The better we can master the skills of improvisational risk, the more agile and adaptable we become.

Operational Risk

Not all risk happens in the moment. We are often engaged in long-term activities that take time to unfold and complete: getting to work each morning, manufacturing a product, performing surgery, preparing a holiday meal. If you approach these tasks with your desired result in mind and see the parts that make the operation run, you can apply risk to change and improve these parts, ultimately changing the results.

Toyota made famous its process of just-in-time (JIT) for assembling cars, which has been adopted by tens of thousands of manufacturing operations around the world. Building a car involves hundreds of steps with thousands of individual actions. To improve the process, Toyota management encourages all employees to communicate ideas and experiment to find better and faster ways to manage each step.[4]

What makes JIT work so well is that the process frees employees to take calculated risks in a culture that strictly adheres to a scientific approach for experimentation. As with jazz, a few critical, culturally structured rules provide Toyota's operations with tremendous flexibility and adaptability. Employees are constantly thinking of ways to push the limits on activities and processes, discussing their ideas, and creating controlled experiments to see how the ideas work. This focus on continual improvement through taking calculated risks by means of controlled experimentation has become the gold standard in most other companies.

Michael Jordan, considered one of the greatest basketball players of all time, realized that age would diminish his power and speed, so he spent years developing both an accurate three-point jump shot and effective low-post moves, which made him a scoring threat far into the latter part of his career. Tiger Woods retooled his swing several times in his career to adjust for changes in his body, equipment, and the golf courses themselves. Taking risk to operationally improve is key to sustainable success.

These examples highlight the power of operational risk. By breaking the operation into its key components, trying new approaches, reducing or eliminating steps, testing wildly different techniques, and continuing to apply pressure to improve results, the workers accomplished something that they would have thought impossible.

Companies can keep competitive by embracing continuous improvement and challenging all rules, processes, and product/service offerings as well as keeping an eye on market and environmental changes and anticipating needed innovations. Here's how you can break down operational risk into its most critical parts:

1. **Focus on your processes.** How does the work actually get done? Start with this exercise. Ask employees to map out their work individually, then have them meet in their natural work teams to trade notes and slide their pieces of the puzzle together. Next, have work team leaders meet with team leaders from other functions to map out the flow of work across functions. Last, pull together a leadership team to fill in the strategic holes and finish assembling the puzzle. All too often managers initiate change only in things they see, while ignoring or considering irrelevant for their attention things they don't recognize.

2. **Identify owners of the processes.** Each process should have someone responsible for its quality and optimal functioning. Although this person leads the processes, he or she must act more as a facilitator for the workers who execute each part of the process. Working in tandem with those who run the process, the process owner can build the agenda, goals, and metrics and run interference on efforts that impede the process.

3. **Give creative permission.** Michael Hammer, a former professor of computer science at the Massachusetts Institute of

Technology and known as one of the founders of the management theory of business process reengineering, has said, "The rubber of operational innovation hits the road at the front lines, where people will have to change what they do on a daily basis and how they do it. For many, this is a difficult and even wrenching experience, and one that they will find all kinds of excuses to avoid. Dropping such changes on them out of the blue will guarantee failure, and preaching to them about the enterprise's financial goals will not help them adjust."[5] It seems obvious that the people who should be most involved in developing new ways of working should be those who are themselves doing the work. Give them permission to develop new ideas that may make the process better. Give people time to think about new ideas, to share them with others for feedback and adjustment, and to demo them in controlled tests to see if they work and how they can be improved. Allow people to fail, as failure is the best way to learn. The results of these ideas should then be shared with the process team to implement the change quickly and efficiently.

4. **Make action your mantra.** It is easy to talk about making change and taking risks. It is another thing to put muscle into it and see it through to the end. In their book *The Knowing-Doing Gap: How Smart Companies Turn Knowledge into Action,* Stanford professors Jeffrey Pfeffer and Robert Sutton share the reasons why gaps exist between what firms know they should do and what they actually do, and why firms fail to implement the experience and insight they've worked so hard to acquire. They encourage companies to build cultures that encourage doing something with ideas and reward workers and management with financial and social incentives for ideas that are acted on. Don't waste good ideas because of the smart-talk syndrome or the it's-not-in-the-budget excuse.[6]

5. **Engage leadership.** According to Hammer, "the finest idea will not get implemented unless there is an organizational

framework for shepherding it from concept to reality."[7] Providing the right incentives, resources, structure, and support to allow people to take risks will go a long way toward shaping a culture that seeks continuous operational risk.

Game-Changing Risk

The Declaration of Independence, the steam engine, electricity, the abolition of slavery, the airplane, the Model T, and the assembly line. More recently, semiconductor devices, the iPod, the iPhone, Facebook, and Twitter. All of these inventions are examples of game changers. Not only were they new and innovative; they changed the way we live our lives.

Game-changing risk is the big, ballsy move that creates an entirely new idea, product, or social movement that can change the rules forever. It can be personal as well, such as the bold decision to run your first marathon, change careers, or start an entrepreneurial venture. It can be about your company, impacting your organization's work at every level, entailing a healthy dose of risk, and marking a definitive turning point for the organization. It is when the phrase "risk versus reward" really comes into play, as the risks and the rewards are elevated much higher, to a level that is often much more public. Subsequently, it's not surprising that this type of risk-taking often creates severe anxiety and that those willing to engage in it are rare indeed.

This type of innovation is incredibly hard for most organizations to do well. It takes a lot of elbow grease to improve what you are already doing or what you are already offering, which is why, later in this book, I introduce a new methodology called improvisational innovation. In improvisational innovation, good ideas in product and process can bubble up from anyone at any time. You don't have to build out the "big I" (game-changing innovation) but rather focus on the "little i" (improvisational innovation) that builds next generations by improving upon what you already have.

Ronald Heifetz, a professor at Harvard University's John F. Kennedy School of Government, notes: "If you make one real decision in your life, that's more than most people. . . . Peoples' choices to take or refrain from risk are over-determined by their culture."[8] How many times have you thought about doing something extremely risky, only to hold yourself back? Why did you?

Not everyone is built with the temperament to become a game-changing agent. This is okay, as every organization can't be entirely full of risk-takers. Every organization needs people to anchor it in turbulent waters and focus on keeping the boat afloat. An organization has to strike the appropriate balance between risk-takers and safeties, those who not only play it safe but challenge the risk-takers in ways that can help mitigate utter failure. Yet organizations without a good number of big-thinking risk-takers are themselves risking someone pushing them to the ground and stealing their lunch.

I believe one reason companies resist risk-taking as a process is that they see it as equivalent to gambling, but it is not. Collective knowledge can greatly mitigate risk itself. The best risk-takers work closely with mentors, and in a team atmosphere where they can explore all possible outcomes with far more security than any individual is likely to have on his or her own. Many of the executives I interviewed for this book, and those for whom I consult, are acutely aware that they desperately need to institute risk-taking as a practice, but almost everyone outside the C-suite believes that if you take a risk and fail, you get fired. And how often are they right? The only true cure is a redefinition of failure, from the top down, declaring that all experimentation is about learning, which is a gain, not a loss.

PART II

The DNA of a
Bold Risk-Taker

Jokke Sommer, a Norwegian who has had a fascination with flying like a bird since he was very young, started BASE (Buildings, Antennas, Span, and Earth) jumping in 2008. Of course, this naturally led to wingsuit flying. If you are unfamiliar with wingsuit flying, the easiest way to describe what it looks like is to think of a flying squirrel. The design of the wingsuit and the trajectory of jumping from a cliff at high velocity and gravity, simply put, enables people with the ability to fly. The best wingsuit jumpers can speed over treetops and through mountain passes at about 125 to 135 mph.[1] "You're using your body and when you jump off you kind of use the acceleration force to make your wingsuit inflate and the gravity is your engine and you have to control your legs and arms and shoulders—it's just kind of like you would imagine flying yourself." According to Sommer, the faster you go, the safer it is, so he prefers to fly at around 155 mph and only about 10 to 12 feet from the ground. "The most important thing is that you stay current and develop an awareness of what you do. . . . Your life gets so much more rich and filled with joy. It's not focused on the money, but focused on the smiles and waking up in the morning and just doing something you love to do," says Sommer.[2]

In a PBS documentary titled *Birdmen: Original Dream of Flight,* Dr. Lester Keller, a sports psychologist, says:

> In most of these kind of [extreme] sports, there's a very small elite group that participates in them. Very few people have the ability to do it—have the courage to do it. To do something really challenging, and really risky, and to succeed at that, there's certainly a reward for people to do something that other people can't do or won't do. I think that drives you to overcome that aversion that most people have. Motivation for some of these kinds of activities, or things that happen by accident, is that they are life-altering

experiences. And once you have done that, and you've had that feeling, I think if it was that profound and that rewarding, you want to do it again.[3]

Bold risk-taking is the difference between living an ordinary life and an extraordinary one. While some people seem to be born risk-takers, it can be learned.

THE GENETICS OF HUMAN RISK-TAKING

Not surprisingly, men, as a whole, are inclined to take greater risks than women. A study by Mara Mather and Nichole R. Lighthall titled "Both Risk and Reward Are Processed Differently in Decisions Made under Stress" found that gender differences are amplified even further under stress.[4] Male risk-taking tends to increase under stress while female risk-taking tends to decrease. One reason for the dichotomy between how men and women are equipped to take risks is that there are differences in brain activity involved in computing risk and preparing for action. In the study, when the genders were presented with a risky decision task involving monetary reward, their behaviors differed. Male participants under stress had greater reward collection and faster decision speed than females, yet women demonstrated more analytical and calculated processing under stress. The researchers concluded that although the study provided a greater understanding of the gender differences in the neural activity involved in stressful decision making, other influences such as genetics, social environment, and personal interactions play a pivotal role.

"Risk Aversion and Physical Prowess: Prediction, Choice and Bias," a study by Dr. Sheryl Ball, Dr. Catherine Eckel, and Dr. Maria Heracleous, academics at Virginia Polytechnic Institute and State University, Texas A&M University, and American University, respectively, concludes that genetics such as physical attractiveness and physical strength affect people's ability to take more risks.[5] While it has been assumed that attractive people are more risk-tolerant, the researchers did not find conclusive evidence to support the assumption. However, they did conclude that confident people are more comfortable taking risks, and a majority of their confident subjects were more attractive. Physically stronger individuals take more risks because they are capable of observing physical cues and incorporating them into their risk-taking forecasts. In addition, the researchers found that participants' self-perceptions affected their risk behaviors.[6]

Both age and height impact who is risk-tolerant and who is risk-averse. The willingness to take risks decreases markedly with age when linked to financial gains and losses, according to researchers from the Institute for the Study of Labor, the University of Bonn, and the German Institute for Economic Research in Berlin.[7] For men, as they age, there is a steady increase in their unwillingness to take risks; women's unwillingness to take risks increases at a rapid pace from their late teens to about age 30 and then remains flat until it increases again from their mid-50s and above. In the study's evaluation of 22,000 respondents, the interviewees were supposed to imagine that they had won 100,000 euros in a lottery, part of which they could invest. By doing so, there was a 50 percent likelihood that they would double the amount invested within two years. However, the risk of losing half the money invested was just as great. When analyzing the results, the researchers report that taller individuals are more willing to take risks because they have greater confidence and better self-esteem due to their height. Through this hypothesis, the researchers find that taller individuals are more likely to have positive economic outcomes, thus increasing their willingness to take risks.

THE MOLECULAR GENE

Often natural risk-taking just boils down to our molecular makeup. *Time*'s Alice Park summarized the work of Dr. David Zald, professor of psychology and psychiatry at Vanderbilt University, writing that "people who take risks get an unusually big hit of dopamine each time they have a novel experience, because their brains are not able to inhibit the neurotransmitter adequately. That blast makes them feel good, so they keep returning for the rush from similarly risky or new behaviors, just like the addict seeking the next high."[8]

Robust dopamine production virtually ensures risk-taking, says Larry Zweifel, a neurobiologist at the University of Washington. "When you're talking about someone who takes risks to accomplish something—climb a mountain, start a company, run for office, become a Navy SEAL—that's driven by motivation, and motivation is driven by the dopamine system. This is what compels humans to move forward."[9] Whenever we accomplish something, dopamine helps us feel a sense of satisfaction; the riskier the thing we've done, the bigger the hit. "Think of dopamine like gasoline," says Zald. "You combine that with a brain equipped with a lesser ability to put on the brakes than normal, and you get people who push limits."[10]

RISK-TAKING IS AS MUCH LEARNED AS IT IS BORN

Like all behaviors, there is a nature-nurture factor to risk-taking. Geography, socioeconomics, gender, age, religion, birth order, whom you surround yourself with, and other influences all can have weighty impact on the risk-takers we do or do not become. You may start out with certain personality attributes, but you are heavily influenced by your environment. Growing up in Miami, Florida, weather played a huge role in my risk tolerance and risk aversion. I personally don't enjoy experiencing hurricanes or late-afternoon thunderstorms, and now I am raising my kids in northern California, where they are scarcely familiar with what rain is, much less thunderstorms. I live in an area where mountain lion sightings are a regular occurrence, so my appetite for hiking—an activity that very much defined me in young adulthood—with my young children has diminished greatly.

Even the amount of chutzpah possessed by a whole generation of people can be affected by circumstances. Andrew Newell, from the University of Sussex, theorized one of the great economic puzzles in history: Why did full employment not lead to inflation in the 1950s and 1960s as it did in the 1970s?[11] Newell believes that workers in the 1950s had embedded memories of the Great Depression of the 1930s, which caused them to fear joblessness and therefore accept low or no pay raises. However, by the 1970s, a whole generation of workers had grown used to full employment, and felt comfortable enough to demand higher pay, with higher inflation being a result. These workers gave birth to new generations who were able to break with norms, have access to much greater information, explore the world with much greater frequency, and really have the opportunity to broaden their perspective on the way things could be. This led to the birth of a new crop of innovators and bold risk-takers.

THE DNA OF BOLD RISK-TAKERS

For this and my prior book, I conducted empirical and qualitative research with some of the world's leading innovators and developed a profile of the characteristics that made them such admired inventors. At the heart of their risk-taking, these innovators:

- Refuse to accept the status quo.
- Are in touch with a much greater purpose in life.
- Focus on products, services, and ideas that emphasize value creation above all else.
- Value talented people and understand how and when to collaborate with them.
- Are able to effectively execute an innovative idea, whether they do it themselves or delegate to a small team of others.
- Can scale their innovation to a level that can affect many.

More specifically, I found that many of these risk-takers share eight core attributes:

1. **They genetically have a lower level of fear than most people (or even an absence of fear).** As I stated earlier, dopamine drives individuals to seek out and learn new things as well as process with great regularity certain emotions, such as anxiety, fear, and excitement. When risk-takers are not getting a proper dosage of rushes, their equilibrium is off, and they can struggle emotionally until they get back to their "normal."

   Risk-takers also have a disproportionate amount of testosterone (therefore, men are more frequent risk-takers); the steroid hormone that plays a role in maintaining muscle mass, physical and mental strength, and energy also helps determine the level of one's risk tolerance. In a *Time* article titled "High Testosterone Means High Profits," author Adam Smith reports that the testosterone levels of financial traders were higher on profitable trading days than on other days, which indicates that increased testosterone levels may cause traders to be more confident and have a bigger risk-taking appetite.[12] However, an increase in cortisol, the hormone that regulates immune response and has a direct correlation to stress levels, often leads to a decrease in testosterone. Researchers found that while rising levels of both testosterone and cortisol allowed big risks, chronically elevated testosterone levels can lead to irresponsibly risky behavior, while extreme cortisol levels can make traders shun risk altogether.[13]

2. **They are creators, not observers.** Risk-takers don't sit around living other people's lives. They are the creators whom everyone else watches, and they will likely create until they are done, rarely taking time off. In the process of creating, they use both sides of their brain. While everyone uses both sides of their brain to process information, it's *how* risk-takers do it that makes them more creative thinkers. Complex cognitive functions require the brain regions to work in an integrated fashion, shifting between divergent

and convergent thinking to combine new information with old and even forgotten knowledge. Most people either feel more comfortable looking at concepts over minutiae, or vice versa, but risk-takers more easily shift between both sides of their brains.

3. **Risk-takers are incredibly curious about why things are the way they are.** Curiosity for risk-takers is an *innate* instinct, and curious people have a hard time accepting the way that things are without thinking about the way things can be. Neuroscientists strongly associate curiosity with attention, motivation, memory, and learning. Based on experiences, uncertainties, and stimuli, curiosity is engaged and practiced throughout one's lifetime. With its openness to foreign experiences, curiosity creates a sense of wonder and imagination and has been linked with cultivating happiness. In his book *Stumbling on Happiness,* Daniel Gilbert, a Harvard psychology professor, makes the argument that many people believe they know what will make them happy in the future, but the reality is that we find more happiness in an unplanned occurrence than in a planned notion.[14] By nurturing curiosity and remaining open to new experiences, risk-takers increase their probability of doing something innovative and naturally finding meaning and relevance in their lives.

4. **They are promotion-focused; they hate losing more than they love winning.** Dr. Nate Kornell, an assistant professor at Williams College, states that psychological research shows that people vary on a continuum called "regulatory focus," meaning that one is either promotion- or prevention-focused.[15] In this case, bold risk-takers are promotion-focused people who thrive on taking chances, comfortably dreaming big, and thinking creatively. They are eternal optimists who plan only for best-case scenarios—unprepared with a Plan B because they wholeheartedly believe that Plan A will work. The worst thing for risk-takers is not to take

the chance. They often hate losing more than they love winning, which is a very important distinction in the mind-set of great risk-taking innovators.[16]

5. **Risk-takers surround themselves with like-minded risk-takers.** Bold risk-takers need to be surrounded by other bold risk-takers, and often they are bored with people who are not similar to them in their risk tolerances. Having a mentor and surrounding yourself with people who inspire and influence you give you the freedom to push the envelope beyond the norm of possibilities and generally encourage bigger and bolder accomplishments.

6. **They believe that anything is possible.** These individuals are fearless about taking on new businesses, sectors, and challenges even when the so-called experts tell them otherwise. They go to any and every extreme to be the best and demand nothing less. They do believe that anything is possible, and no obstacle is too large or insurmountable because their passion for the end result overcomes any hesitation.

7. **They can shake off and even embrace failure.** Bold risk-takers redefine what failure is. It has nothing to do with losing. Failure is a learning opportunity, and in certain environments, such as Silicon Valley, it is redefined as a positive and is embraced, because it means that risk-takers are now smarter and they'll have a sense of what to do and what not to do next time. At worst, failure is seen as a speed bump.

In the chapters ahead, this book details how you can learn to be a deliberate and strong risk-taker within any organization, government entity, or nonprofit in the areas that can have the greatest impact within any organization: leadership, corporate culture, talent development, innovation, intellectual property, smart work, decision-making, brand and marketing, and sales. There are examples of risk-taking from past and present, examples of heroes and heroines who are bold characters and have made the big bets. At the end of each chapter, a section called "The Risk Factor" reveals some of the best organizational risk-taking practices that you can adopt or modify to fit your organization. Whether you are a C-suite executive, an entrepreneur, a mid-level manager, a government employee, or just starting your career in a nonprofit, this book will illustrate how to zig when everyone else wants to zag.

Go into this book recognizing that without risk, we do not grow.

CHAPTER TWO

Bold Character Leadership

People who don't take risks generally make about two big mistakes a year. People who do take risks generally make about two big mistakes a year.

—Peter F. Drucker

On April 13, 2013, Jeff Bezos, founder and chief executive of Amazon, sent a letter to shareholders that reinforced his company's ethos: customers, investment, and, above all, long-term value creation should come first, even at the expense of shareholder returns.

Bezos has a simple life philosophy—commission is better than omission. What he means is that when we are 80 years old and look back over our lifetimes, our biggest qualms are likely to be omissions—all the things we wish we had accomplished in life. Bezos envisions all life moves, large and small, in the context of a "regret minimization framework."

Putting his ethos into practice, Bezos knew that if he didn't try to involve himself in the Internet in some big way, it would haunt him every day. "You know, I left this Wall Street firm in the middle of the year [to start Amazon]. When you do that, you walk away from your annual bonus. That's the kind of thing that in the short term can confuse you, but if you think about the long term then you can really make good life decisions that you won't regret later," Bezos said in a May 2001 interview with the Academy of

Achievement, a nonprofit that brings together extraordinary leaders with promising youth to inspire them to succeed.[1]

In June 1994, Jeff and his wife, MacKenzie, flew to his parents' home in Fort Worth, Texas, while he mulled over the most opportune city for his new company.[2] He settled on Seattle because there was already a bustling tech scene, with companies such as Microsoft, Nintendo, and RealNetworks, so it offered a great pool of programming talent. It was also only a six-hour drive from America's largest book distribution center, the Ingram Content Group, in Roseburg, Oregon. This would allow the new Internet bookstore to offer nearby customers the rare and, at the time, new experience of same-day and/or overnight service.

Living in New York, Jeff and MacKenzie had never owned a vehicle, so Jeff's father, Miguel Bezos, gave him the keys to his six-year-old Chevy Blazer. While MacKenzie did most of the driving to Seattle, Jeff sat and typed Amazon's first business plan on his laptop. The couple settled in Bellevue, a Seattle suburb, where they rented a three-bedroom ranch house with a garage that had been converted into a family recreation room heated by a potbelly stove. Amazon was born in July 1994 in that converted garage.

Bezos's bold bet was that Amazon could cut prices to give its customers the lowest price and win their deep-seated loyalty at the expense of short-term profitability. Wall Street analysts were aghast; these were the days when business models had yet to be disrupted by the Internet. In the eyes of investors, Bezos's moves had relatively low odds of paying off. Amazon continuously confounded Wall Street analysts, who were baffled by the risks Bezos took. Irrespective of Amazon not being very profitable and despite all the doubts, the company became one of the most valuable businesses in the world—a business that no one else has been able to replicate. Bezos's commitment to long-term value creation remains steadfast. His April 2013 letter to shareholders begins in this way:

> As regular readers of this letter will know, our energy at Amazon comes from the desire to impress customers rather than the zeal

to best competitors. We don't take a view on which of these approaches is more likely to maximize business success. There are pros and cons to both and many examples of highly successful competitor-focused companies. We do work to pay attention to competitors and be inspired by them, but it is a fact that the customer-centric way is at this point a defining element of our culture.

One advantage—perhaps a somewhat subtle one—of a customer-driven focus is that it aids a certain type of proactivity. When we're at our best, we don't wait for external pressures. We are *internally* driven to improve our services, adding benefits and features, before we have to. We lower prices and increase value for customers before we have to. We invent before we have to. These investments are motivated by customer focus rather than by reaction to competition. We think this approach earns more trust with customers and drives rapid improvements in customer experience—importantly—even in those areas where we are already the leader. . . . Our heavy investments in Prime, AWS, Kindle, digital media, and customer experience in general strike some as too generous, shareholder indifferent, or even at odds with being a for-profit company. . . . To me, trying to dole out improvements in a just-in-time fashion would be too clever by half. It would be risky in a world as fast-moving as the one we all live in.[3]

On April 14, 2013, a *Business Insider* article observed that "many other promising companies that rode the Internet wave have stumbled, in part because they put too much emphasis on short-term profitability and failed to invest enough in long-term value creation. (Think AOL, Yahoo, eBay, Microsoft, and, most recently, Apple.)"[4] The world's obsession with short-term profitability (often shortsighted concern for shareholders) is what will kill innovation. William Lazonick, of the University of Massachusetts Lowell, as summarized by Eric Reguly, suggests that CEOs should be wary of shareholder demands for instant gratification. "The trend to reward shareholders with lavish buybacks benefits the sellers, not the long-term owners, and deprives companies of the resources to fund

R&D, train employees, make acquisitions, and engage in other activities to improve productivity and competitiveness."[5]

Bezos's bold spin on the traditional business model, putting profitability behind customers' happiness and loyalty, forever changed how organizations define, create, and deliver value. Customer happiness not only became his guiding north star, but it set a standard for how all decisions would be made moving forward by asking, "What would make the customer happy?"

Traditional definition of leadership:	The action of leading a group of people or an organization.
Risk-taker's definition of leadership:	Helping someone or something grow. Characterized by imaginative energy, a strong sense of self-assurance, ingenuity, and dedication to an endless journey.

THE WORLD CALLED ASKING, WHERE ARE ALL THE BEZOSES?

There is nothing more fundamental today than bold, character-driven leadership—that is, if an organization wants to survive. Without leadership, you don't set the right corporate culture; without corporate culture, you won't attract the best people; without the best people, you can't effectively innovate. Most forward thinkers I've interviewed do not believe bold leaders exist in incumbent business. You can, however, find them in the technology world, but otherwise, they are few and far between. In leadership, it is business as usual. The question is: Why is this so? Why can't traditional leaders evolve? In all fairness, it is far easier to build bold character leadership from the ground up than to inherit someone else's organization and the remains of a predecessor's leadership style. Then again, bold leadership is an anomaly in the incumbent world largely due to the way boards of directors have become beholden to their institutions. First, consider a CEO's tenure. According to a *Harvard Business Review* article titled "CEOs Should Get Out of the Saddle before They Are Pushed Out," a Fortune 500 CEO spends about 4.6 years in that position; other CEOs serve about 8.6 years.[6] No matter how experienced an incoming executive is, it takes time to decipher who is who and what is what. Even with the best and boldest of intentions, in complex and bureaucratic organizations, it can take years to figure out how to be effective, and by the time most CEOs figure out how to impact the bottom line, it is time to go. How can CEOs think of and execute a strategy for long-term value creation when they face boards of directors, shareholders, and, inevitably, Wall Street analysts who breathe down their necks about daily stock prices and short-term profitability? Boards of directors want an affable, easy-to-work-with CEO. The CEO has to spend more time being liked by their board, shareholders, and people than challenging the norm or working toward the seemingly impossible. It is like running for president of the United States; the moment you take office, you have to start the reelection process.

Second, if you are going to serve as CEO for only 4.6 years, then why not milk the company for as much compensation as possible? "Chief executives of the nation's largest companies earned an average of $12.3 million in total pay last year [2013]—354 times more than a typical American worker, according to the AFL-CIO."[7] Do average Fortune 500 CEOs really think that their value is so much greater than the people who generate new ideas or revenue or cost savings for the company?

Third, among incumbents, it is all about ownership for the few and the mighty: who has the biggest this and that and who owns the most. It is the twentieth-century idea of leadership and management that has never matured. In contrast, in Silicon Valley, as I mentioned earlier, there is a belief that everyone contributes to the success or failure of the organization, so equity ownership is shared across the organization. After all, if you are part of the value created, why wouldn't you benefit proportionally? Most people in Silicon Valley believe that this is the region's fundamental value proposition, where no one has an insignificant stake in the outcome of a venture, which leads to much greater gains in the long term.

It takes a bold character leader to stand up, change the formula, and do the right thing. Paul Polman, CEO of Unilever, is one of the few bold leaders at a traditional Fortune 500 corporation. In 2009, when Polman took over as CEO, he decided to eliminate quarterly profit reports, refused to give earnings guidance to analysts, and informed hedge funds that he would not be humored or lured into trying to meet their expectations. Unilever was his business to run, and Polman's view—that "shareholder value" is hobbling American-style capitalism—makes him an outcast in modern management circles. In a 2013 *Globe and Mail* article, Polman states that it is time to put an end to the cult of shareholder value. "The very essence of capitalism is under threat as business is now seen as a personal wealth accumulator. . . . We have to bring this world back to sanity and put the greater good ahead of self-interest."[8]

LEADERSHIP IS NOT MANAGEMENT

Bold characters and risk-taking leaders put the mission and the goals of the organization ahead not only of their own self-interest but of that of their shareholders. It is not about power, money, or ego but the pursuit of results. Then why don't the majority of leaders take risks? The answer is simple: Because it feels unsafe, and security, for most people, is more important than anything else. Managing tasks and processes well is easier than leading people to greatness. Most executives get confused between what it means to lead and what it means to manage. In our era, leaders of organizations are asked to manage, and managers are asked to lead. The push and pull of these often conflicting responsibilities has created confusing issues for leaders and workers alike.

The science of management says that we have to dehumanize the human. There are behavioral parameters to which the leader and the manager have fallen prey. Leadership pioneer Warren Bennis, in his book *On Becoming a Leader*, outlined the often conflicting attributes of management and leadership:

- The manager administers; the leader innovates.
- The manager is a copy; the leader is an original.
- The manager maintains; the leader develops.
- The manager focuses on systems and structure; the leader focuses on people.
- The manager relies on control; the leader inspires trust.
- The manager has a short-range view; the leader has a long-range perspective.
- The manager asks how and when; the leader asks what and why.
- Managers have their eyes on the bottom line; leaders have their eyes on the horizon.
- The manager imitates; the leader originates.
- The manager accepts the status quo; the leader challenges it.
- The manager is the classic good soldier; the leader is his or her own person.
- The manager does things right; the leader does the right thing.[9]

I suggest one more item for this list:

- The manager shuns risk; the leader encourages risk-taking.

The missing ingredient of bold leaders today is risk-taking. This is true of both the risks you take and the risks you don't. Few people want to be led by someone who doesn't take risks. This lack of risk-taking in leadership is what is destroying organizations. If you think the death of Kodak Eastman was a fluke, just wait. Traditional incumbents will continue to lose market share, tap out on future growth, or become obsolete if they don't start to make big bets with the potential for big payoffs. Just ask Louis Gerstner.

One of the boldest risk-taking leadership moves in history was that of Louis V. Gerstner Jr., known as the man who saved IBM. Taking the reins as CEO in 1993, Gerstner walked into the largest computer company in the world. Yet it was about to go under. At the time, IBM had revenues of $62.71 billion, but its net income was a *negative* $8.1 billion,[10] and Gerstner had inherited a flat PC business, a piecemeal software business, and a mainframe business (IBM's claim to fame) that had been in a death spiral for years. Due to earlier leadership, IBM was locked into selling IBM products only, which severely crippled the company's ability to best serve its clients. Between 1991 and 1993, IBM lost a staggering $16 billion. The once "most admired" company was fast becoming a has-been.

So what did Gerstner do first? He forced the company into solvency through substantial layoffs, eliminating billions of dollars in expenses. Gerstner's next order of business was to put a stop to a proposal that was already in the works to break up IBM into various operating units. He characterizes this as "the most important decision I ever made—not just at IBM, but in my entire business career."[11] Gerstner wanted to use all parts of IBM—hardware, services, and software—to deliver well-rounded technology solutions. Within his first year as CEO, Gerstner traveled worldwide, visiting customers, analysts, and industry specialists to learn from them firsthand. "They said repeatedly, 'We don't need one more disk drive company, we don't need one more database company or one more PC company. The one thing that you guys do that no one else can do is help us integrate and create solutions,'" says Gerstner.[12]

Instead of concentrating on building even bigger and better PCs and mainframes, Gerstner cut against the grain by declaring that IBM would turn itself into the largest IT consulting company and systems integrator in the world. It would sell competitive products and acquire outside product lines to bolster its position as the premier source for an organization's holistic IT needs. In a speech to Harvard MBA students in 2002, Gerstner said, "Transformation of an enterprise begins with a sense of crisis or urgency. No institution will go through fundamental change unless it believes it is in deep trouble and needs to do something different to survive."[13]

IBM employees could feel the ground rumble. Since Gerstner inherited IBM, he spent a significant amount of time and resources assessing the culture, seeing who would be capable of buying into his vision and who would not be. Gerstner decided to motivate employees by providing financial benefits based on the performance of the whole company, not just a single division. The purpose was to encourage employees to work together, collaborate, and think outside the walls that surrounded them.

Gerstner's bold bet paid off handsomely, and today IBM is indeed the world's largest IT consulting company.

THE MIND-SET OF BOLD CHARACTER LEADERS

At the beginning of the twenty-first century, the world started to see a new crop of leaders, like Gerstner, who were driven by results and who genuinely wanted to contribute to the greater good. Jeff Bezos, Steve Jobs, Larry Page, Sergey Brin, Elon Musk, and Mark Zuckerberg were all driven primarily not by money but by a guiding principle to disrupt the way that things are traditionally done and seek pathways that would provide benefit to everyone. Their driving passion and brilliant execution also happened to bring them fame and fortune. What sets them apart from the incumbent leaders whose main objective is to please shareholders, boards of directors, and their bank accounts?

First, the leaders mentioned above understand that willingness to take risks is at the very heart of their leadership. Period.

Second, and most important, is how bold leaders see themselves and view their role compared to their peers. From the empirical research I conducted, I have become captivated by the dichotomy between the mind-set of innovators on the West Coast and that of executives I knew living on the East Coast. West Coast leaders see themselves not as CEOs at the helm of some big empire but more as chief innovation or product officers, still in the trenches with their peers and continuing to tinker on projects themselves. They know how to shift between being coaches and team players. They act on a good idea as a team, give credit where due, and genuinely want to see their team and everyone around them succeed, so they give motivation and support. They recognize that no longer are senior leadership opinions the end-all; good ideas can come from anyone at any time, regardless of age, gender, or pay grade. By incorporating viable ideas and creativity from all ranks, they become an integral element in helping someone or something *grow,* as opposed to managers who are preoccupied with getting something *done.*

Third, they engage in conversations of "Yes, and . . . ," a concept that I go into more deeply in the Improvisational Innovation chapter. By having "Yes, and . . ." conversations, they get the best out of their people by encouraging not squashing anyone's ideas, realizing that there are good ideas that produce immediate results and others that may not work, but the dialogue ensures that every voice is heard. Elon Musk, for example, offers any full-time employee at Tesla the opportunity to meet with him directly, provided they have a well-fleshed-out idea in a written proposal. Paul Jacobs, the current executive chairman and former CEO of Qualcomm, invites people to walk up to him to share interesting ideas. NetApp CEO Tom Georgens told me that he constantly thinks about how he can learn about good ideas from the people who actually do the jobs. Larry Page, cofounder and CEO of Google, gets out of the way of people who can contribute value and doesn't pretend that he has all the answers. I don't see these behaviors in the incumbent world. What I see is CEOs who travel with entourages just so people can't walk up to them.

Fourth, bold leaders are concerned far more with long-term value creation than with short-term profitability. What makes Intuitive Surgical, a Silicon Valley–based surgical robotics company, so innovative is not just the product it sells but the man at the helm, its CEO, Dr. Gary Guthart. Known around the office for his humble demeanor, Guthart prohibits employees from ever mentioning the company's stock price, requires everyone to fly coach, irrespective of the distance they must travel, and asks them to always think of the company as a start-up. Guthart rarely agrees to speaking engagements or media interviews. He feels that if takes his eye off the ball—which is delivering the best robotic surgical instruments possible—then the company shouldn't be in business.

Finally, these great risk-taking leaders still rely on a mentor. They don't make a decision in a vacuum; rather, they surround themselves with a circle of smart people, build coalitions, and minimize the overall risk. When billionaire entrepreneur Mark Cuban was told that he takes great risks, Cuban disputed the charge, stating that he doesn't take any risks because his decisions are based on his knowledge and experiences and the people he surrounds himself with to vet ideas.[14] Sir Richard Branson, founder of Virgin Group, always talks about turning to a small cadre of mentors when he plans new ventures. According to Branson:

> Mentoring was very important for me personally. For example, Sir Freddie Laker [an airline entrepreneur who is now deceased] gave me invaluable advice and guidance as we set up Virgin Atlantic, while my mum has been a mentor throughout my life. Nowadays, I find mentors inside and outside of Virgin every day. If you ask any successful businessperson, they will always have had a great mentor at some point along the road. If you want success then it takes hard work, hard work and more hard work. But it also takes a little help along the way.[15]

THE RISK FACTOR

The bar for bold character leadership today extends far beyond having an MBA from a leading university. In addition to being a great manager of people and process, you have to have a general knowledge of technology, an artist's creativity, an anthropologist's sense of people's rhythms, and a humanitarian's concern for people.

Be a Technologist

We live in heady times, accelerating at an exponential pace. Technology has now surpassed our own brainpower. In an IBM release titled "New IBM SyNAPSE Chip Could Open Era of Vast Neural Networks," IBM reveals that their scientists have created the most neuromorphic (brain-like) computer chip to date. Called TrueNorth, and consisting of 4096 cores, 1 million neurons, and 5.4 billion transistors, it is the product of almost a decade of IBM research. TrueNorth mimics the functionality of the brain in software and applies this knowledge to hardware intended to partake in a specific task. This technology would allow for processing of sensory data in real-time in "a context dependent way," and open up new possibilities for mobile, super-computing, computer vision, AI (self-driving cars), and personal or wearable computing. Ray Kurzweil's 2005 fictional book *The Singularity Is Near,* in which "our intelligence will become increasingly nonbiological and trillions of times more powerful than it is today," is quickly becoming more reality than fiction.[16]

You can no longer have your head buried in your organization or be completely reliant on a technologist to help determine your short- or long-term strategic planning. James Manyika, the director of the McKinsey Global Institute, states, "The reason disruptive technologies are very important to all leaders—whether they're CEOs or policy makers—is because, for the first time, we now have technology affecting every single sector of the economy. Every sector, whether it's retail, financial services, shipping, manufacturing, and even agriculture, now takes inputs and uses technology to drive much of what it does."[17] This agility is crucial in a world where new competitors and new markets pop up every day. No one can take that for granted, not even the leaders at Google. Susan Wojcicki, now CEO of YouTube, formerly led Google's ad products and confessed that she obsessed over keeping up with new technologies being created on a daily basis outside of Google.[18]

On top of this, leaders across industries must now think of their firms as technology companies first. "Savvy business leaders understand risks well enough to see past them and envision the massive opportunity in transforming their business with data-rich social and mobile apps, powered by comprehensive analytics, enabled by the agility of cloud computing," says NetApp's cloud czar, Val Bercovici. "If Dunkin Donuts' CEO Nigel Travis sees *his* company as primarily a technology company which happens to serve coffee and donuts, shouldn't every other mainstream business leader leverage technology to reinvigorate core growth in their own markets?"[19]

Be an Artist

Creativity is one of the most important attributes in risk-taking leadership, and it is a characteristic that leaders should look for in others when building out their teams. In the 2010 IBM survey called "Capitalizing on Complexity," which surveyed 1,541 corporate and public sector leaders in 60 countries and 33 industries, creativity was identified as the most important leadership quality, outweighing integrity and global thinking. Creativity is what enables leaders to think outside the box, break away from the status quo of their industry, and tap into thinking beyond the products they build into areas such as human behavior. Creative leaders can rethink their products, processes, and business models when necessary, and if they are creative enough to dream and execute on those dreams, they can reinvent their enterprises. But we still divide the world into creative and noncreative types and therefore don't capture the comprehensive talent of the organization. And by failing to encourage creativity among "noncreatives" we deny organizations (and society) more creative people. It starts at a young age.

The chair of the U.K. government's report on creativity, education, and the economy, Sir Ken Robinson, described research that showed that young people lose their ability to think in "divergent or non-linear ways." Of the 1,600 children (aged 3–5) tested, 98 percent demonstrated an ability to think in divergent ways. But by the time they were aged 8–10, only 32 percent could think divergently. When the same test was administered to 13- to 15-year-olds, only

10 percent could think in this way. And when the test was given to 200,000 25-year-olds, only 2 percent could think divergently. "Education is driven by the idea of one answer and this idea of divergent thinking becomes stifled."

Robinson described "creativity as the 'genetic code' of education and said it was essential for the new economic circumstances of the 21st century."[20] The good news is that people don't lose the ability to be creative, they just lose practice. As we grow older, we get more self-conscious, and we worry about being judged. Consequently, how do you enable creativity so that great ideas make their way into the hands of people who can use them? Two things need to happen:

1. **Blocking and tackling.** Hierarchical command and control common in many corporations has to be broken down.
2. **Creative activity.** Open-mindedness has to be fostered.

Here's a simple, three-step way to practice creativity. I go into greater detail regarding some of the elements in subsequent chapters.

Step 1. Make Time
First, stop thinking that "play" time is an indulgence. Play provides the best learning opportunities, a chance for people to clear the clutter and think about things differently. There is a direct correlation between playful experimentation and innovation. Second, schedule a specific time each week to concentrate on a creative project—new thinking in process or product development.

Step 2. Get Out of the Office and Inspire New Thinking
Set a timeline for when your team can inspire new thinking and brainstorm. Whether it is once a week or once a quarter, take your team out of the office, preferably to open spaces where people can think and reflect from varying heights and different vantage points. Square founder and CEO and Twitter cofounder Jack Dorsey likes to take his team hiking around San Francisco Bay. It not only gives

people perspective and fosters new ideas for innovation and processes but also allows them to get to know one another beyond the day to day of being in the office. Brainstorming works best when peers really know one another's personal hobbies and interests and can draw on them to enhance brainstorms.

Step 3. There Is No Failure in Creativity

Inhibitions have got to be checked at the door, and colleagues need to realize that something that appears to not work on the surface may provide the path to what could work. No idea should be thought of as crazy, and everyone should start from the perspective that anything is possible. Dr. David Crawley, a semiconductor physicist and an expert in lean methods, learned the hard way when building out the Robotics Hacker Dojo in Mountain View, California. "The minute I discouraged people in their ideas, I inevitably realized that they would not return." What Crawley realized is that he needed to suspend his disbelief and realize that all ideas have some applicability to some meaningful outcome. "The worst thing you can do is discourage people from executing their ideas, and I had to learn that there is no failure in creativity."[21]

Be an Anthropologist

When Yahoo! CEO Marissa Mayer was head of search products and user experience at Google, she noticed that some members of her team were off kilter; employees just were not as productive at given times of the day throughout the week, so she decided to take a poll. She went to her leadership team and asked, "What's your rhythm?" and got a variety of responses. Mayer wanted to find out what was on their minds, what they felt they were missing out on, where they'd rather be on different days and times throughout the week. What she found was perfectly in line with human nature: Her employees could give even more if they had certain designated times to spend with family and friends. One female engineer responded that she wanted to be at her daughter's soccer game on

Thursday afternoons at 4:00 pm and to have dinner with her family thereafter. Mayer responded, "Done!" So, every Thursday Mayer mandated that this employee leave the office by 3:30 to enjoy that time with her family. A male engineer said that he wanted to be with his college friends on Tuesday nights when they all gather for dinner. Again, Mayer responded, "Done!" and made it very clear to the rest of the team that both employees were not to be contacted during personal time unless it was an absolute emergency.[22]

Once it was clear that her staff had a better balance of time spent, Mayer found she had a happier and more productive team. "I believe it really meant a lot to my staff that they were heard, they were valued, and that we were secure enough to look at their overall productivity and not their face time," says Mayer.[23] Finding people's rhythm is now a common staple of Mayer's leadership—in spite of what you might have read about her calling back telecommuting Yahoo! workers. Mayer insists that is a different issue altogether. In fine-tuning a particular company's needs, she says, productivity and creativity are maximized when people are brought together but continue to respect each other's individual rhythms.

Be a Humanitarian

"I never saw Bill Gates happy until he started to give away his money," Marc Benioff, the chairman and CEO of Salesforce, remarked when he was being honored on September 26, 2013, for his giving at the annual Churchill Club Awards dinner, a leading Silicon Valley business and technology forum that fosters conversations on the latest technology and cultural trends. "Why should he be the only one happy?" Benioff asked.

When Benioff started Salesforce in 1999, giving back was going to be deeply ingrained in both the culture and the strategy from inception. He instituted the "1/1/1 model," a simple formula that consists of donating 1 percent of company equity, 1 percent of his employees' time, and 1 percent of his product to improving communities around the world. "When it comes to philanthropy, I have one pitch, and it's been the same since the founding of our company," he said.[24]

Fifteen years later, Benioff is a man of his word. In the midst of his world tour to promote Salesforce1, a social, mobile, and cloud platform built to transform how companies sell to customers, the company was simultaneously holding a food drive in the lobby of the New York Hilton in Midtown Manhattan for the more than 1 million New Yorkers who face hunger each year even though the social issue had little to do with Saleforce's core business.

Benioff also created the Salesforce Foundation and divided it into three categories: people, technology, and resources. According to the company website, the foundation has become a "social" social enterprise, "an organization with a sustainable business model, driven by a social change mission, with community engagement for social good at its core." "Since our founding, we have given over $68+ million in grants, and 680,000+ hours of community service, and provided product donations for over 23,000 nonprofits."[25] By promoting a culture of caring and helping employees to give back, offering donated and discounted technologies to nonprofits, and providing grants inspired by Saleforce employees, technologies, and communities, the foundation's strategic efforts support communities where employees live and work. For the people part, each year every Salesforce employee is allowed up to six days paid time off for volunteer projects of their choice. The technology piece is Salesforce's "Power of Us" program, which gives nonprofit organizations and higher education institutions access to and discounts on Salesforce products and resources, thereby aligning with the firm's core competencies: people, products, and profits. And the resource strategy includes elements like Force-for-Change grants, which focus on increasing collaboration through the global nonprofit sector. In North America, for example, the foundation funds the development of technology solutions that help communities achieve their social change missions more efficiently.

Giving is very personal for Benioff, as it was something he and his wife vowed to do back in 1999, provided Salesforce was highly successful (it grew to $4 billion in revenues in 2014). At the Churchill Club Awards dinner, Benioff said that he was giving away their wealth for these four reasons:

1. It is easy to do.
2. It is massively impactful.
3. Lots of organizations need it.
4. Those who can, must.[26]

CHAPTER THREE

The Corporate Culture of How

On August 31, 2013, speaking at the Churchill Club, Tom Georgens, the CEO of NetApp, a leading data management and storage company, stated something that few leaders have the courage to admit: "It wasn't a failed vision of leadership, but it was a triumph of our [NetApp] culture." What Georgens was referring to was a

$1 billion idea that came not from leadership, but from the ranks of NetApp's 12,000 worldwide employees.

Around 2008–9, the need for efficiency in data management was beginning to be felt deeply. Companies found their IT costs skyrocketing and were buying more servers to keep pace with their ever-growing data. The market was in a transitive state and demanded more efficiency in the datacenter and more powerful processing and IT infrastructure. NetApp field teams noticed different trends coming together and recognized that it could culminate in the perfect opportunity for NetApp and its partners.

The company had worked with Cisco on a joint architecture for secure multi-tenancy, a shared infrastructure that can securely run multiple workloads independently, each with their own quality of service requirements. The core NetApp team working on the project felt the need to package the architecture to make it easily definable, quick to deploy, and much easier for customers overall. The team then proposed an idea to their Cisco counterparts (the two companies are occasional strategic partners when they need to offer specific IT requirements in next-generation virtual data centers) that would take advantage of the market's pressing need. The idea was to explore an architecture for server, storage, and networking components that are pre-tested and validated to work together as an integrated infrastructure stack. When NetApp and Cisco joined forces on this project, they offered customers the ability to improve the utilization rates of their infrastructure, shorten the deployment time for new applications, ease infrastructure management burdens, and reduce the risk of downtime. By November 2010, the two companies had launched "FlexPod."

The team also devised a new plan to take the product to market: Since they did not have the resources to try direct sales as a go-to-market means for FlexPod, they had to get creative and do more with less. They recognized that there was a potential to have channel partners play a bigger role in the sales process. If sales for the product were led by the channels, then not only would NetApp have an army of people behind the product, but the diversification would give channel partners an additional revenue source. Both sides would win with a stronger relationship, and FlexPod would have more scale and extended geographic reach.

These ideas didn't come from formal planning. They came from a large group of people that identified the need in the market, felt empowered to do something about it, and collaborated to make it happen. The team's confidence and passion kept them going through obstacles, and while they didn't have many resources, the culture of the company allowed them to chase down their idea, invest time and effort into it, and make it a success. The company's leadership did not pour money into the project, but they did stand up to support the team's endeavors.

FlexPod has generated $3 billion in joint sales since its launch in 2010.[1]

How did four NetApp employees have the freedom to just dream up and execute FlexPod? "The real advantage of our culture is not only that you have happy people but that our culture helps our employees to have the freedom to inspire people to create innovative products or processes that help customers win," says a marketing manager in NetApp's Global Communications department. "If NetApp had a bureaucratic culture, ideas like FlexPod would never materialize, because they would never make it to the point of ideation."[2]

Not every employee at every company has to focus on the next billion-dollar idea. Success can have different meanings to different companies, such as: Do we produce a great product? Do we provide the best service? Are we profitable? What do we want to be known for? Is our work important to the greater good? The answers to these and other questions help define what a company thinks of itself. Successful companies rise above the fray by doing exactly what they want to do, and doing it very well. However, company culture is not just about what you do but *how* you do it. Every company culture is different, and each needs to focus on not just what they do, but how they do things. This is the promise of what I call the *Culture of How*.

A CULTURE OF HOW = TRUST + AUTONOMY + RISK + KNOWLEDGE SHARE + IMPROVISATION

Around Silicon Valley, NetApp has the reputation of being a place where people love working. The company has won several "Best Places to Work" awards. In 2014, *Fortune* magazine named Net-App to the "100 Best Companies to Work For" list in the United States for the twelfth consecutive year.[3] NetApp has also been consistently featured on the esteemed "World's Best Multinational Workplaces" list by Great Place to Work®.[4]

I was truly fortunate to be allowed to take a deep dive into NetApp's culture for the research of this book, and in subsequent chapters I share examples of how its autonomous culture has enabled other innovations. Roaming through the halls of NetApp over a period of nine months, I found energized people who act less like self-interested employees and more like family members who share a common passion to help the company win. I wanted to figure out why people loved working at NetApp, and why its culture was unique with regard to how they get work done. Here's what I discovered.

NetApp has a blueprint for how a company should operate in a socially connected economy. The company mantra is about how employees get things done, not what they do as a data storage company. It is a carefully crafted balance of how employees and teams operate. To me, its Culture of How looks something like this (note that the descriptions and allocations of time are my own observations, not NetApp's):

1. **Work together.** We should swim in the same lanes (approximately 75 percent of the time).
2. **Pursue independent passions.** Stay in your own lane and swim in your own path (approximately 20 percent of the time).

3. **Tackle overlapping or competing interests.** If different groups are competing on similar projects, We need to stop and figure out how to best collaborate or identify how to take the lead (approximately 5 percent of the time).

Autonomy, trust, risk-taking, knowledge sharing, and continuous improvement are at the heart of NetApp's Culture of How. An autonomous culture allows people to be passionate, self-inspired leaders, makers of their own destiny. "At NetApp, there is flexibility to make decisions if you have to . . . having that mandate inspires leadership and initiative among most any employee," says one of the company's marketing managers. In fact, when CEO Tom Georgens speaks to new employees during his T.O.A.S.T. (Training on All Special Things) orientation—a "unique one-day orientation program designed to help all new employees learn about the culture, values, strategy, organization, and norms of NetApp"[5]—he tells each new hire that they have the ability, freedom, and responsibility to differentiate NetApp—in other words, anyone is given the autonomy to change the future of the company. Georgens is also quick to point out that NetApp has been doing a great job attracting people who are not in the business solely for their own enrichment, but who work with each other to move the company forward while making it the best professional experience of their lives. "It speaks volumes that the founders of NetApp are still active members of the team. They're still talking to customers, sharing feedback with me on what they hear," Georgens says. "If you treat people with respect and allow them to have autonomy, chances are that they are more likely to enjoy what it is that they are doing and that makes for a better customer experience."[6] He believes that by paying attention to your customers' needs and not your competitors', you can make products that solve customer challenges in a differentiated way.

NetApp has developed the right mix of daily productivity, innovation, risk-taking, and pursuit of employees' passion projects. The company's Culture of How is neither hierarchal nor flat but operates more in what I would describe as a circular fashion, through which ideas and their execution evolve in interdisciplinary channels. In NetApp's case, waves of ideas continuously flow from the company's employees to internal and external stakeholders, growing stronger as they move along, so that the ultimate collective punch is much more powerful than a solitary proposal. Improvisation is an accepted part of the process, and the value of an idea is at NetApp's cultural core. For example, when a senior marketing manager at NetApp first had an idea to take the company's best customers to the Formula One race in Austin, Texas, she initially had some pushback from some colleagues on the value and cost of the experience. NetApp is an extremely relationship-driven company, so the senior marketing manager decided to "swim in her own lane" and vet the idea with other divisions. She was able to draw the interest of NetApp's cloud czar and built a coalition of support that then won over her own team members. The senior marketing manager said, "I've worked in other tech firms where you could never pursue a passion or idea once your immediate team nixes it."[7] The full story of the Formula One event and the bottom-line value it had for NetApp is discussed in The Era of Collaborative Sales and Customer Service chapter.

NetApp is a culture of "Yes, and . . .": Ideas are not squashed, so people maintain their enthusiasm for raising new ideas. This process requires improvisation, leadership, and support where appropriate, in addition to give-and-take. As you riff on an idea, your colleagues support you and prepare to build off the result even if initially they may not agree with it. Everyone understands that the long-term goal is to create profit, whether it is financial, social, whatever. Employees respect and trust each other. They understand that someone else birthed the company, but they are all in it together to raise the child, watching it grow up; they know the value of the Culture of How.

WHY CORPORATE CULTURE
MATTERS MORE THAN EVER

- *91 percent of executives agree that "culture is as important as strategy for business success"*
- *81 percent of executives agree that a company without a winning culture is "doomed for mediocrity"*
- *Fewer than 10 percent of companies succeed in building one.*

—from Bain and Company[8]

The most common complaint I hear among corporate executives in Silicon Valley is that they have a tough time competing for top talent (especially among female engineers) when up against the Apples, Facebooks, Googles, NetApps, and Netflixes of the world. What I tell these executives who are not part of one of these companies is as follows:

Corporate culture is the single greatest differentiator of an organization's success.

And if they don't offer a strong corporate culture, one that appeals to the multigenerations now in the workforce, then they will never attract the best and brightest. Culture drives and shapes everything an organization does. It impacts every aspect of the "three Ps" (people, process, products)—from employee hiring and behaviors to customers' attitudes. Today it is not enough to sell something; you have to *stand for* something. And of course, the "cool" factor is essential for the millennial generation of talent, whether it is in the social currency in the products you make or the free-flowing work environment you provide. Companies like Apple, Facebook, Google, NetApp, and Netflix have personalities and souls, and they also foster autonomy, collaboration, and freedom. The talent you attract today will dictate where your future lies. The idea of culture being a key differentiator is so simplistic, but so many organizations resist evolving a strong culture or don't know how to.

Brian Halligan, CEO of HubSpot, a marketing software platform, argues that "99% of companies are kind of stuck in the '90s when it comes to their culture."[9] For centuries it was thought that elite Europeans (and eventually Americans too)—those with civilized upbringing, superior education, means of global travel, and the resulting high-brow perspective—were the only individuals fit to run things. This elitism permeated government, charity, and corporate governance. The average Joe was not trusted with high-level decision making, as he lacked the pedigree and the connections to do the proper thing.

A radical cultural change has taken place over the last two decades, though. Because of the increased speed of work, the explosion in the amount of available information, and the means to communicate globally, companies have been forced to hand some of the decision-making reins to the growing "knowledge workforce." In today's world, top talent is embraced for being more independent, knowledgeable, and creative than earlier generations were, and for expressing their unique traits in the workplace. This type of talent is not interested in being stifled by micromanagers,

Traditional definition of corporate culture	Culture is the accepted norms and behaviors of a group of colleagues and makes up a key component of an organization's strategic direction.
Risk-taker's definition of corporate culture	A unique personality and soul based on shared values, passions, and authenticity. The culture guides the norms and behaviors of employees to create a shared employee/customer mind-set for bottom-line results.

deferring to snail's-pace processes, and receiving annual raises that don't reflect the value they can bring to an organization. Nor are they interested in corner offices, being on a higher floor of a building, or beauty contest dressing. This type of talent is more interested in throwing on a T-shirt and getting things done. Most organizational leaders are ill prepared for, and reluctant to accelerate, this change. Little do they realize they are having their lunch stolen from them right in the middle of the schoolyard, and they have no means of fighting back.

WHAT IS YOUR CULTURE?

Going back to my open space tree analogy in the introduction, when I am brought in to to speak to organizations, I frequently begin my talks with this question: "If I say the word 'tree,' what kind of tree do you visualize?" Someone might say maple tree, another cherry, oak—even cactus. I share with my audience that I visualize a palm tree, more specifically, the Canary Island date palm. I have been living in Silicon Valley for eight years, and palm trees are not necessarily what you think of when you think of northern California—a redwood or sequoia would come to mind. But it was my first 17 years growing up in Miami, Florida, that defined my vision of what a tree is. It was these memories of childhood in the late 1970s and early 1980s—searching for coconuts and trying for hours to crack them open—that are most deeply imprinted in my mind.

Usually each person in the room mentions a different tree, depending on their experiences—where they grew up, memories, likes/dislikes. I can take a simple word like "tree" and, in a room of 25 colleagues, get 25 different answers. Continuing on with the exercise, I ask them to think about the word "culture" in the context of their own company, and I scribe on a whiteboard the myriad of responses: Just because they all work in the same environment doesn't mean they have the same understanding of their company's corporate culture, particularly if one has not been set by the leadership and deeply communicated to employees and practiced throughout the organization.

A SHIFT IN VALUES

Some people believe that today we live in a binary economy that has adopted the free market and people's right to property but strongly encourages reform of our existing banking system. When I was a graduate student of macroeconomics, I bought in to the neoclassical definition of Adam Smith's laissez-faire style of the free market, which is based on an economic environment that is free of government regulation and is fair and efficient—a market where you could supply a product and there will be demand for it. This neoclassical definition now seems woefully out of date because the theory doesn't account for social behaviors. In my opinion, our shifting values have given us far more control over our destiny than generations past had. Because of this, I believe there is an element that has to be accounted for when it has a great impact on the consumption of goods and services, and that is *values*.

We entered this century with a tremendous amount of fear. Our 24/7 multimedia cycle made it nearly impossible to avoid the negative news. Prior to the turn of the twenty-first century, we panicked about Y2K, and then came 9/11, thereafter a mortgage crisis, and massive unemployment, and then the Great Recession, and so on. But oddly enough, the fear brought our values to the forefront. We were forced to reflect on how we lived our lives versus how we wanted to live our lives. We were forced to do our work and seek out what made us happy. It even changed our shopping habits. American cupidity was put on pause (the spendthrift decade of the 1990s suddenly seemed an embarrassment). A sharing economy started to look acceptable, even attractive, and necessary to save the planet. Those lucky enough to have employment choices wanted to work for companies whose values matched their own. Employees no longer wanted bosses; they wanted coaches, people they could partner with.

Customers and clients also wanted to buy and do business with companies whose values stood for something meaningful. And, more interestingly, they suddenly wanted to be a part of a community, preferably one that offered social currency. Apple products, for example, fueled that desire. Carrying an iPhone says something about who you are and connects you not only to your generational peers but to everyone who shares your passions and value system, whether they are 17 or 71 years old.

We now want to live and work in environments that are consistent with our values. This atmospheric shift is, in part, why corporate culture is the single greatest differentiator of our times.

GOOGLE: IN THREE WORDS

Included in the 2004 IPO prospectus, the letter from Google cofounders Larry Page and Sergey Brin to potential investors stated that Google's workplace atmosphere and management philosophy would depart from that of any other organization ever built. The letter laid out their vision for the company and their commitment to safeguard that founding culture even decades later. It stated:

> Google is not a conventional company. We do not intend to become one. Throughout Google's evolution as a privately held company, we have managed Google differently. We have also emphasized an atmosphere of creativity and challenge, which has helped us provide unbiased, accurate and free access to information for those who rely on us around the world.[10]

Google fulfilled its promise to become unlike any other company. It made nerdy techies cool, brought people's outside lifestyles into the workplace, and created, in my opinion, the ultimate culture of creativity and innovation. From Google's inception, the cofounders wanted transparency where everyone was "in the know." Page and Brin created TGIF ("Thank God It's Friday"), a first-of-its-kind open forum, where employees have the opportunity to ask the cofounders anything. According to the company's website, in the first 30 minutes of the meeting, Page and Brin "review news and product launches from the past week, demo upcoming products, and celebrate wins," but the second 30 minutes is Q&A from the employees, without any fear of retribution. (Everything from the trivial to the ethical is up for debate.)[11] Page and Brin believe that this is the optimal way to provide an open forum of openness, so that employees can apply themselves in ways that management often can't anticipate.[12] Of course, it is much harder to be this closely connected when you have nearly 50,000 employees around the globe, but my point is that from the get-go, Page and Brin were acutely cognizant of how their unique culture needed to embody every aspect of the Culture of How.

When I speak to corporations about what makes a strong corporate culture, I always use Google as a case study. I begin by showing Google's logo on a slide and asking the audience: "If you had to describe Google in three words—either by looking at the logo or by your perception of what the company stands for—what would you say?" Inevitably, I get answers like "colorful," "innovative," and "search." I don't agree that all of these concepts are actually reflected in the company's logo and branding, but I have nearly 100 percent participation from my audiences—all using similar words—which means that just about everyone has a clear idea of what they believe Google to be; they often know it better than their own corporate culture. I throw all the suggested words into another slide but bold three words—colorful, quirky, and fun—that set the foundation of cultural norms both internally at Google and externally through the customer experience.

Then I ask my attendees to break into small groups and offer up three words that describe their culture. Nearly every person I have spoken to at almost every company is perplexed when they try to do this exercise. Most have been indoctrinated in some bureaucratic mission statement, yet they are incapable of repeating it—because there is usually nothing worth repeating. So, we embark on a brainstorming session of sharing ideas, words, and phrases that they would like their organizational culture to be. It takes a bit of laughter and rolling up of sleeves, but it's an important first step in a company's culture exploration.

CREATING A RISK-TAKING CULTURE

There is no doubt that culture can affect a firm's appetite for risk and consequently its risky corporate decisions. By supporting people's differences and individual passions, and by raising the level of trust, you foster the type of risk-taking that drives superior corporate growth.

Why is a risk-taking culture good for a corporation? In the technology industry, with a vast landscape of unexplored possibilities still open, the fastest path to success is failing often and failing quickly. The lessons learned from failure are extremely valuable for making good business or technical decisions in the future. It is equally important to ensure there is no culture of fear or blame. Fear of failure or scapegoating can kill innovation in any company, big or small. In fact, publicly recognizing those risks that didn't pay off and the lessons learned will reinforce this desirable behavior. Take an honest look at how you deal with failure. It will help enable a risk-taking culture if managers of the organization themselves exhibit risk-taking behavior, demonstrate failure, and make lessons learned from failure public. One employee at a leading pharmaceutical company even suggested that failures should be kept in an open-source database, with examples of who took the risk, failed, and kept their job.

It is unrealistic to expect innovation if risk-taking is suppressed by the corporate culture. The mandate for a risk-taking culture needs to come from the top and be adopted at all levels. A company serious about promoting risk-taking behavior would be wise to coach employees on "smart" risk-taking—to act when there is a probability of a high payout for a low investment, even with a larger probability of failure than otherwise. These lessons should emphasize knowledge, limiting the downside and catching failures early in the cycle. It is critical to redefine how we think about failure, as we are always learning in the process and the information gained can either mitigate future risk or be the conduit for other innovations. By creating a safe environment and offering appropriate incentives, you can improve staff morale and encourage the culture you desire.

THE RISK FACTOR

Create a Culture of How

A Culture of How is the best way to make sure your workforce is fully prepared to handle the new realities of work and to focus not on what you do but on how you do it. To achieve this cultural transformation and allow for the adaptation of internal cultural risk-taking processes, consider taking the following steps.

Step 1. Do a Cultural Audit

First, you have to know where you stand: Just what *is* the perception of your culture? How do your board of directors, executives, employees, and trusted clients and customers describe your culture? Disseminate a short survey asking, "If you had three words to describe our corporate culture, what would they be?" or "What brand outside of our company do we think we (or want to) embody?" In the process of gathering this data, allow people to answer honestly without any fear of retribution. If possible, gather the data anonymously through an outside source, so that it's unfiltered. In the end, share the data with your team so that you can set a tone of openness and transparency.

Step 2. Relinquish the Emotional Attachment to the Past and Reestablish Your Values

Now more than ever, the pace of change demands scrapping even the most cherished products, services, and projects. Even once-brilliant ideas will not necessarily stay relevant to your employees, customers, or clients for years on end. Clearly stating your values allows employees more permission and support to take necessary competitive risks. Just state what you mean, such as Google's values statement, which begins "Don't be Evil"; while Volvo, highlights "safety."

My all-time favorite is from Craigslist, which states:

- Giving each other a break, getting the word out about everyday, real-world stuff;
- Restoring the human voice to the Internet, in a humane, non-commercial environment;
- Keeping things simple, common sense, down-to-earth, honest, very real;
- Providing an alternative to impersonal, big-media sites;
- Being inclusive, giving a voice to the disenfranchised, democratizing; and
- Being a collection of communities with similar spirit, not a single monolithic entity.[13]

A values-based culture fosters an environment in which employees can be trusted to do the right thing because they know what the organization stands for. Chick-fil-A is a great example of a company that has stood by its value proposition since 1946, when founder Truett Cathy made the decision to close its doors on Sundays. Cathy believed that Chick-fil-A operators and their employees should have Sunday as a family day and a day to rest or worship if they so choose. Sixty-nine years later, the company not only didn't cave on that commitment but expanded its values-based directives to employees and customers. Drive up to any Chick-fil-A, and you will find dedicated parking spaces for employees and drivers of clean-air vehicles (in closest proximity to the restaurant), employees who come out from beyond the counter to deliver your food, serving containers that are mostly biodegradable, and paper crafts for kids (rather than plastic toys) that inspire imagination and creativity.

IBM had to move from a viewpoint of "IBM products first" to "the best interests of our customers first." This simple values shift meant gutting decades of products, distribution, marketing, and sales processes and reinventing the company's value stream. After making the shift to becoming an IT consulting firm, Gerstner spent almost two years traveling the world, speaking to internal IBM audiences to sell them on his vision for the future and educating them on the new value system. He made it clear that if each individual made the voluntary effort to make the new vision succeed, he or she would find a bright future with IBM. If people felt they were not up to the task, that the change would be too uncomfortable for them, IBM would help them with the search for their next job outside of the company. Gerstner knew that IBM could not succeed by holding on to employees who did not share the company's new vision and values.

Step 3. Appoint Cultural Ambassadors

Changing minds is a marathon, not a sprint, and fatigue and doubt often hamper things. An appointed cultural ambassador can elevate the level of authenticity, build trust and the relationship between employees and management, and highlight the issues most important to employees. Ambassadors help stay the course and can provide real-time employee feedback on top issues and concerns, act as cultural change advocates, and meet periodically with other employees to discuss transformation issues. An ambassador can be a volunteer or chosen by management, or even an employee who already acts as a corporate evangelist. Hewlett Packard (HP) launched a voluntary pilot program where management nominated 445 cultural ambassadors throughout the company who served as trusted connectors who embraced change. Each ambassador then assigned a local senior leader to meet in person with the ambassadors monthly to ensure that everyone was communicating similar messages about the culture but simultaneously respecting the cultural norms of HP's locations around the world. In other words, what works in India doesn't necessarily work in China, so the ambassadors would make modifications based on cultural norms and sensitivities, depending on the global office they sat in.

Step 4. Align Your Workforce

In order to execute a successful cultural shift, you need to reset your processes around decision-making, talent development, and incentives. Much of this is discussed in subsequent chapters. You have to recognize that people fear the unknown. If you want people to adopt a Culture of How, you have to offer incentives and a way to measure results. Gerstner realized that IBM's new approach demanded a new set of rules and a new set of skills. To drive change, IBM began rewarding teamwork—although Gerstner learned that it wasn't enough. "People don't do what you *ex*pect but what you *in*spect," he says. As a *Forbes* article relates, he therefore "created a new way to measure results. Employees needed to know that their competitors were outside of IBM, not across the hall. Secondly, there would be no more 'obsessive perfectionism' and 'studying things to death.' In the new IBM, people would be rewarded for getting things done fast."[14] Before Gerstner went to IBM, he believed that culture was just one among several important elements in any organization's makeup and success, along with vision, strategy, marketing, financials, and the like. However, "I came to see, in my time at IBM, that culture isn't just one aspect of the game; it is the game. In the end, an organization is nothing more than the collective capacity of its people to create value."[15]

Step 5. Promote Internally and Seek External Input

Leaders cannot operate in a vacuum and need to stay current with outside suggestions from customers and employees. Hands-on outreach to customers can help spot potential issues before they cause inconsistencies. Also, setting up ways to channel feedback will support overall momentum. On the employee side, people want to feel both secure and excited about the future—you want a cultural mandate to energize them, not scare them off.

Equally important to a successful execution, explore the opinions of customers you work with and those you do *not* work with. Find out what they think of you, no holds barred.

You should take this a step further by periodically taking the temperature of customers in industries that you do not sell in. Seeking out opinions beyond your immediate industry will provide a snapshot of the strength and reach of your brand, as well as your standing in the world of customers.

Tell Your Culture in a Narrative or Storied Promotion

Mark Crumpacker, CMO of Chipotle, said in a 2012 *Fast Company* interview that they tell their customers what's really inside their burritos. "Typically, fast-food marketing is a game of trying to obscure the truth."[16] Crumpacker wanted the world to know about Chipotle's sustainable "Food with Integrity" message. According to the article, Crumpacker put on various screenings of the undercover documentary *Food, Inc.* He discovered that the best way "to differentiate Chipotle was to replace traditional advertising with more emotionally engaging stories," Crumpacker said. "If a company like that [Chevron] can make you cry, imagine if we had something comparable for Chipotle."[17]

The short animated film *Back to the Start,* produced by CAA for Chipotle Mexican Grill, graphically depicts a farmer's unsettling adoption of factory farming before switching to a sustainable practice of turning animals out to pasture. The film was released on Chipotle's YouTube page in August 2011, then played in over 10,000 movie theaters during the fall. Then the company turned it into its first national commercial. The two-minute ad debuted during the 2012 Grammy Awards telecast, and viewers were encouraged to download the song, a Willie Nelson rendition of Coldplay's "The Scientist."

Chipotle "devised its marketing approach based on its own research, which showed that 75 percent of its 800,000 daily customers came for the taste, value and convenience of its food."[18] The company wanted to get customers more passionately involved, and in order to do that, it had to tell its story in a more emotional, human way.

CHAPTER FOUR

The Death of HR and the Birth of Talented People

David Rudman, director of talent for IDEO's Bay Area locations, never imagined a career in human capital management. He thought he'd take a year off after undergrad to work at a Silicon Valley law firm and see if law school was the right fit for him. It wasn't, so he took a contract job at Google in 2007, sourcing candidates for software engineer positions. Since I was aware of the fierce battle for top talent, particularly among Google, Apple, and Facebook,

I was curious about the rumors of astronomical salary packages for Google engineers, who allegedly are paid far more than those at rival Silicon Valley firms.[1] Rudman couldn't answer, because that was someone else's responsibility. "All I did was source potential engineers from specific schools and companies that Google favored," Rudman told me. He wanted to play a broader strategy role in the talent side of people, so after a year at Google, he sought out another opportunity.

When David Kelley, the founder of IDEO, wanted to start a design firm and innovation consultancy in 1991, he wrote to his friend Dennis Boyle, asking him to join. The letter essentially conveyed that Kelley was planning to start a new firm and wanted his best friends as his first employees. Who wouldn't want to be surrounded by their best friends on a daily basis, in an environment of mutual trust and respect? After 23 years in business, IDEO is still a "very human-centered-culture," where its number one internal priority is to create an amazing employee experience. After all, Kelley believes, that's how you'd treat your friends.[2]

Rudman knew that IDEO was the type of workplace he wanted to be a part of, where people are happy and engaged in a firm that emphasizes opportunities to grow in knowledge and leadership. "First, we are a small shop and a very flat organization, and we don't have a ton of [human resource] policies . . . in fact, we have very few," Rudman told me. IDEO's HR department is made up of four professionals in Palo Alto and another six globally for the 600-person firm. "If you put a lot of policies in place, then you don't allow people to have freedom, and it runs completely counterintuitive to everything that IDEO embodies."

In addition to generous compensation, performance bonuses, and other broad financial benefits, such as company- and studio-specific profitability, IDEO has a simple and unique approach to growing talent: Allow people to engage in projects that they actually want to do. A "talent lead" is designated in each of IDEO's five groups (digital, product, brand, systems and organizational design, and internal process) who acts as the "mom" of the group and whose primary responsibility is the professional talent development of every employee in the group. And being human-centric, these talent leads celebrate birthdays, recognize when employees are stressed out and need personal or professional support, and serve as sounding boards for what's going on in their employees' lives. To fill these roles, IDEO brought in counselor types who had served as chief happiness officers at start-ups like Watku, an organization that focuses on building strong corporate cultures and increased employee engagement. IDEO was also the first design firm to seek out "T-shaped people," defined as those who have a depth of expertise in one area and a broad base of interests and passions in other areas, but do not necessarily have a depth of expertise in the group discipline in which they are working.

IDEO projects vary in length from a few weeks or months to, in cases of strategic partnerships, years. Because of the ebb and flow of projects, the talent leads anecdotally accumulate knowledge of what the people on their team want to do next. If a mechanical engineer, for example, has been working on a project for a Fortune 100 company and wants to work with a smaller entrepreneur next, every attempt is made to ensure that happens.

"It is about hiring the right, curious, and highly engaged talent in the first place, and allowing them the freedom to explore personal passions as well," Rudman explained. Of course, when you hire such curious people, often their appetites can take them in a myriad of directions. Sometimes IDEO employees get so involved in a project with a client that they want to see the project they prototyped go to market (and may end up joining the very company that IDEO contracted with). Others may have personal projects they're developing alongside their day jobs. IDEO strives to find a balance, allowing employees to carry out their entrepreneurial passions with the firm's support. One IDEO employee, Adam Vollmer, on a leave of absence during the writing of this book, designed an electric city bicycle that he hopes will revolutionize the way we think about transportation. He did so on IDEO's property but after the workday, so IDEO owns a small percentage of equity in the business. The company, Faraday Bikes, debuted in the summer of 2013. It remains to be seen whether Vollmer will return to IDEO.

Traditional definition of talent development	The process of changing an organization, employees, stakeholders, or groups of people within the organization using training methods in order to achieve and maintain a competitive advantage for the organization.
Risk-taker's definition of talent development	The nucleus of a formal risk-taking process. Partner with and invest in your employees, treat them well, and allow them the freedom and autonomy to be creative and follow their passions.

THE DEATH OF HR

When your firm employs several hundred people, as IDEO does, you can take high risks fairly consistently. When you are an organization of tens of thousands of people, many company leaders feel that they have to operate predominantly like a machine so that they can mitigate risk. In spite of this, the nature of work is changing, and there is an environmental shift that is greatly impacting the company as we know it—this is all due to more companies, more opportunities, more knowledge workers, and more technologies— and yet we are living in an era where we are all being asked to act in real time. Therefore, we can't continue to fumble through the bureaucracy that the HR world has come to define.

Entrepreneur magazine defines HR as "the department or support systems responsible for personnel sourcing and hiring, applicant tracking, skills development and tracking, benefits administration and compliance with associated government regulations."[3] HR professionals have to negotiate the labyrinth of issues regarding hiring, training, attendance, behavior, purchases and re-source requests, safety, healthcare, compensation and benefits, and much more. Because of the endless legal ramifications and safety concerns, HR has been largely consumed with minimizing risk and exposure to criminal charges, civil lawsuits, and regulatory pen-alties that are brought to the department frequently. Through no fault of its own, HR has become the bad guy.

Mark Zuckerberg, cofounder and CEO of Facebook, had a simple mission: Connect the world. To do so, he needed incredibly talented people who had the right attitude. This nontraditional, strengths-based approach to hiring—hire the best talent, then worry about finding the right role for them—required a company culture that favored flexibility over structure and fostered extreme levels of creativity, adaptability, and risk-taking. Matt Cohler, Face-book's fifth employee, says: "We were determined to keep things as flat as possible. The harder we make it for people to invent to-gether, the faster we fall behind."[4] Because of this philosophy, Face-book mandates that all engineers and operational talent work at its Menlo Park, California, headquarters. There are a few sales offices around the world, but that's it. Keeping engineers under one roof is one of the ways in which Facebook maintains a pioneering culture.

For several years Zuckerberg went without an HR depart-ment, a function he abhorred. He believed that HR professionals would only shave the edge off the very behavior he had nurtured at Facebook—pushing boundaries to generate change and growth. Is this an unfair assessment from one maverick entrepreneur, or is this the tipping point in the war to radically change HR?

Instead of surveying the competitive landscape to find huge talent-related opportunities, today's HR departments spend much of their time saying no to things. This is one reason why HR pro-fessionals never become CEOs.

Edward Lawler, a business professor at the University of South-ern California and an acclaimed HR expert, reflects, "I interviewed a CEO a few years ago who called HR the 'BPU or Business Pre-vention Unit.' He complained that his HR executives were good at identifying what not to do, but were poor at identifying what should be done to make the company more profitable."[5] One chief technology officer (CTO) after another that I interviewed for this book griped that HR continues to block the people they want to hire—in the areas in which the CTOs are experts. One Fortune 100 senior VP of Corporate Strategy, who asked not to be identified, wanted to know the answers to these questions: "If I am responsible for my profits and losses and am showing great results, why do I have to deal with HR, which often has opinions on who and when I can hire? . . . Why do I have to consult with HR when I want to bonus someone? . . . Annual reviews are a time-suck, so why do I even have to do them?" In other words, this senior VP wanted to know why he couldn't just be left alone and judged on his overall performance.

This is not surprising, since most HR departments still work under the mandate that all employees should be treated equally, that their actions should fall within acceptable rules, and that they should follow established procedures. In other words, the job of these HR professionals is to move *abnormal behavior to the normal*. This objective works well for highly efficient organizations built to operate in relatively static environments, such as accounting or nuclear power plants, but not when you are seeking innovative growth.

WHERE DID HR GET OFF COURSE?

In a December 2013 article on a job website called TimesJobs.com (based in India), Aparna Sharma, country head of HR at Lafarge India Pvt. Ltd., discusses the talent vacuum in HR. According to Sharma, a career in HR is not the typical destination for an MBA graduate. Upon graduation, Sharma was consistently asked what field she was going to pursue.

> Instantly the next question was, in what, Finance or Marketing?
> It is assumed that MBA in HR is for those who want work-life
> balance—do not have the stomach for "real" business. And, of

course, a favorite line: "If they're so interested in helping people, why don't they just go into social work? . . .

There is a very famous slogan that is used in all companies "People are our greatest asset!" However, it is difficult to believe in it as only few HR professionals show true commitment to developing and leveraging those people's abilities which has created a bad image of the HR fraternity.[6]

Why doesn't top management share accountability for the HR department's limited vision? The answer is simple: Because top management has allowed behaviors to exist in the HR function that it would never allow in any other part of the organization. HR has grown into the gatekeeper of all things process—payroll, benefits, healthcare, training, and so on. It manages menial tasks and is not creative in thinking. Yet executive leadership has allowed, even enabled, HR to grow more than it ever should have.

The question is: Why?

Leaders want to move forward; they want to do stuff that is fun, even hard, and they don't want to ever be the bad guys, so they pass that off to HR. They ask HR to focus on tasks that have little to do with growing revenue or creating new products. For the most part, HR has grown into "the other side" of the organizational tug-of-war, pulling the rope toward the safe end. HR has been subjected to decades and decades of process overlaid with more decades and decades of process. Its function has been reduced to saying "no," and it has become the greatest mitigator of risk-taking.

But what happens if your markets shift or the nature of work changes and you need to adopt nimbler, more adaptable business practices? And what if you want to take this a step further, angling to disrupt your organization, your industry, and maybe even society? Will HR inevitably handcuff your efforts, or could it become a key partner in the effort? If you ask the Mark Zuckerbergs of the world, the answer should be a wake-up call for HR departments everywhere.

THE BIRTH OF TALENTED PEOPLE

When I ask "What keeps you up at night?," nearly every CEO replies with this question: "How do I innovate?" The conversation before we got to this point goes something like this:

Me: Tell me about your people.

CEO: What do you mean?

Me: Who are your best idea people? Tell me about them.

CEO: (pause) Well, we've got a CTO who's really smart . . . and I am thinking about hiring a chief innovation officer.

Me: Fantastic. How do they spend time outside the office?

CEO: I think my CTO ran a marathon recently, or was it a sailing race?

Me: Okay. What about other people within your ranks and throughout the organization . . . who's got good ideas?

CEO: Ah, I don't know.

Me: How many risk-takers versus risk-averse people do you have among your leadership ranks?

CEO: Ah, well, Dawn is a hell of a risk-taker. Actually, I don't know what you mean, but let me tell you about this great product we have coming out.

THE PROBLEM

Here's the problem: For so long, all companies and their leadership teams cared about was the products they created or acquired. Leaders are deeply dialed into every minutia of the company's products, but not much at all on their people.

THE SOLUTION

How do we learn more about the talents of our people so that we can create the environment to innovate? First, we need to take a step backward and evaluate who is in our workforce. In other words, what are our employees' behaviors, expectations, and ways of viewing the world? Can you create one broad statement that characterizes the three generations—Baby Boomers, Generation X, and Millennials—that are currently in the workforce? I can't, and here's why.

A tumultuous clash occurred when Millennials entered the workforce. It was a blending, like oil and water, of three unique generations that have dissimilar behaviors and expectations about home and the meaning of work. I have chosen a few data points and cultural influences (with a sprinkling of my own commentary) to reference the vast dichotomy between one generation and the next.

BABY BOOMERS

Generally born 1946 to 1964

As kids, they were:

- Children of the Greatest Generation but influenced by the Vietnam War.
- First generation to grow up with television (*black and white to color: the first national color broadcast was January 1, 1954, but it was only in 1972 that color TVs surpassed black and white*).
- Music listeners of the Beatles and Motown (*mostly through transistor radios*) and viewers of Dick Clark's *American Bandstand*.

As they grew up, they participated in:

- Apprenticeships at workplaces.
- Social causes, such as the antiwar movement, civil rights, and the sexual revolution, and lived through the Cuban Missile Crisis and the Cold War.

They are the **Social Cause Generation.**

GENERATION X

Generally born between 1965 and 1977

As kids, they were:

- Children of Baby Boomers; because their mothers had high participation in the workforce, many became latchkey kids who returned home from school to an empty house.
- First generation to grow up with cable TV, leading to more and more viewing choices.
- Music listeners of punk rock, grunge, and hip-hop and viewers of MTV.

As they grew up, they participated in:
- Internships in the workplace.
- Opting out of the traditional workforce, particularly highly educated women.
- Entrepreneurship/Freelancer: Individual effort and business risk-taking.
- Coaching their kid's baseball team, especially fathers.

They are the **Independent Generation.**

MILLENNIALS

Generally born between 1978 and 1995

As kids, they were:
- Wrapped in bubble wrap and received a trophy for showing up.
- Coddled by Mom and Dad, who took care of most of their problems.
- Products of financial crises, but still have a massive combined spending power of over $170 billion annually.
- Viewers of reality television and YouTube videos.
- Music listeners of boy bands, Britney Spears, Eminem, Justin Bieber, Miley Cyrus, and commercially packaged musicians.

As they grew up, they participated in:
- Digital technology, which became ingrained in their DNA: 80 percent sleep with their cell phone next to the bed. Four out of every five Millennials use a smartphone compared to two out of three 35- to 54-year-olds and two out of five of those over 55. Millennials' "average monthly voice minutes have plunged from about 1,200 to 900 in the past two years. Texting among 18- to 24-year-olds has more than doubled in the same period, from an

average of 600 messages a month two years ago to more than 1,400 texts a month."

As they grew up, they:
- Want to be CEO tomorrow.
- Delay rites of passage into adulthood of leaving home and entering the workforce (housing prices are considerably higher than their school debt and entry-level salary can accommodate).
- Consider wealth one of the most important attributes.
- Get married later.
- Have a strong sense of local community.

They are the **Entitled Generation.**[7]

What happens when you mix these generations all together?

Social Causes (Baby Boomer) + Independent Spirit (Generation X) + Entitled Generation (Millennials) = KAPOW!

In my opinion, Baby Boomers and Gen Xers got along okay in the workforce. Gen Xers had very different views of what home life looked like but were still hard workers committed to doing what it took to get the job done. It wasn't until the Millennials came into the workforce at the turn of the twenty-first century that the pot started to stir. Millennials did not understand what the rules of the workforce were, and why should they? This generation had a deep understanding of their importance in the world, and here's what I mean: When you have a technology question at home, whom do you turn to? Your spouse? Unlikely. Chances are that you are going to your kids. In some respects, kids have become the smartest people in the household. Then they enter the workforce, and they are wondering why they can't engage with the CEO and have to go through a chain of command. They are so much smarter academically and technologically, yet we ask them to keep their mouths shut.

Soon after Millennials entered the workforce, the repercussions of overparenting became apparent. The generations started to really see their respective differences and resented what each generation stood for. All of a sudden organizations were at a loss for how to accommodate the variances between the generations, and the wheels began to fall off the wagon—most everyone was challenged by how to get along, how to talk to one another.

The generations learned that they shared almost nothing in common with regard to how they behaved or how they achieved results. Yet the generations do have one thing in common.

At about 19 years old, we all had to figure out what we wanted to do when we grew up (about when we had to think about establishing a major in college). Now, I ask, did you know what the heck you wanted to do at 19 years old? Most people are just getting their sea legs to explore the world around them. Nevertheless, we are forced to select a major at 19 years old, and it then dictates our path in life . . . for the rest of our lives.

So, what do you do? You end up declaring a major based on what your parents or perhaps what your friends do. Here's a hypothetical scenario to prove how ridiculous it is to get a college degree in something you are not likely right for. Your dad is an accountant, so you get a degree in accounting. Say you land your first job as an accountant. Do you love it? Do you even *like* it? It doesn't matter, because chances are you and the rest of the world will peg you as an accountant for the rest of your life.

But what happens if, 15 years down the road, you're married with a mortgage, have two kids, and cannot entertain the thought of going back to school. Spending much more time on the home front, you read an article in *Popular Science* magazine on how to homebrew a basic robot, and it inspires you. It gets your juices flowing, a feeling you have not had since your wedding night. You start tinkering around in your garage. A few years later, not only have you become quite a brilliant hobbyist in robotics, but you invent a new robotics navigation sensor that responds to fluorescent light—something that no one in your company has figured out, but it is something that is pertinent to your company.

What do you do? To whom do you turn? Do you go to your manager whom you don't trust? You decide to go to an engineer in the chief technologist's office (perhaps you are not aware that there is a robotics team or you are aware, but the team is based in India). Now, with all due respect, you are an accountant, and you look and dress like one (I'll leave the physical characteristics up to your imagination, but envision the conservative suit.) The engineer looks like a teen dressed for lounging on the couch (visualize Mark Zuckerberg)—someone who has not showered in a few days. You assume he is a whiz kid, and about half your age. There is nothing remotely apparent that you have anything in common. You attempt to engage in conversation but realize you can't. You give up, and the organization has lost an opportunity to harness your brilliance, all because you got an accounting degree.

Now, back to the CEO's original question: "How do I innovate?" First, read this Risk Factor, then proceed to the next chapter on improvisational innovation to find out how to identify the next big ideas in your organization.

THE RISK FACTOR

Once the organization starts to put people, not products, first, then HR becomes the nucleus of the risk-taking process because it is in the best position to do so, as it is the only part of the organization that touches every other part. HR alone has the ability to transcend organizational boundaries and create partnerships along multiple levels. But this can happen only if the structure of a company allows it and if the CEO is a strong partner. Just describing what a risk-taking culture looks like, telling employees to be risk-takers, and adding it as an objective in an employee performance evaluation document doesn't work. It never has. You have to be able to execute an HR reset.

Let's start with the premise that the HR team is fully functional, having consistently demonstrated its alignment with and understanding of the goals of its leaders, the internal business imperatives, and the external competitive landscape. We'll assume that the HR department itself has the leadership and talent to carry out the mission. If this isn't true, it is imperative that HR go back and get that straight first. It's hard to lead on something that's not embedded in one's own function. This Risk Factor addresses four areas ripe for a reset: HR's own talent, department restructuring, employee development, and policy elimination. And this reset is, of course, also the best way for the HR department to save itself from extinction.

If You Want HR Departments to Think and Act Differently, Hire Risk-Taking, Outside-the-Box Thinkers for HR Roles

Not long ago, talent had to be deeply specialized to fulfill a specific role, but in a knowledge economy, it's to everyone's benefit to be more broad-based and renaissance. In addition to the need for STEM (science, technology, engineering, and math) skills, HR professionals are going to have to seek T-shaped people, a term first described by David Guest in a 1991 editorial about the future of computer jobs but popularized by Tim Brown, the current CEO of IDEO.[8]

Aparna Sharma, the head of HR for Lafarge India whom I mentioned earlier, believes that "HR today sits smack-dab in the middle of the most compelling competitive battleground in business, where companies deploy and fight over that most valuable of resources—Workforce Talent." She sees a major transformation within the function of HR. Instead of being a function that is chiefly about administration, HR will have to shift to maximizing the value of human capital. How do you build organizations where the best want to work, where worker mobility is increasing, and the need for "fulfilling work" is as important as the next promotion? According to Sharma:

A new kind of HR professional is emerging to manage this transformed function, someone who deeply understands not only talent-management processes but also an organization's strategy and business model—someone who is responsible for, say, hiring and training marketing managers but who also knows how to put together an effective marketing plan. Thus, HR professionals are now expected to know not only about their function but also about the business in detail and be true "business partners."[9]

The new HR generalist will have the heart of an entrepreneur, looking for all opportunities to exploit talent to drive high levels of performance and innovation. Change is more dependent on mindset and culture than on specific skills. In both new hires and current employees, the HR professional should seek and grow certain behaviors, such as the ability to ask tough questions, to communicate a clear vision, to lead by example, to build trusting relationships, to execute from knowledge, to be patient yet persistent, and, most important, to curate a different perspective.

In a globally competitive marketplace, HR's new role is to ensure that every position throughout the organization has the opportunity to take risks. What can business leaders do to help HR make the leap? How can HR attract the best talent to work for itself? Think about exploring the following steps.

Step 1. Divide Human Resources
HR has been allowed to grow into a peculiar mishmash of responsibilities. If there is a true dedication to convert HR into an enabler of the risk-taking process, then we need to break apart HR as we know it. Therefore, all compensation-related issues should become part of finance, and all policy, regulatory, and legal issues should migrate to public affairs and/or legal. Simply put, this will allow the money people to handle employees' economic issues and the legal people to oversee the rules. This will free up the rest of HR to focus on the development of its human capital.

Step 2. Create a Chief Talent Development Officer Position
Create and hire a chief talent development officer (CTDO) who sits in the C-suite and reports directly to the CEO. The CTDO's seminal responsibility is to bind talent issues to the organization's business strategy. In order to execute the strategy effectively, the CTDO should fully engage with other C-suite executives in its planning and execution. To fill particular HR needs, the CTDO should recruit T-shaped talent leads who are also knowledgeable in other functions, such as finance or marketing. For example, the talent lead for marketing would have an expertise in marketing, and passions and interests in many other areas.

Step 3. C-Suite Must Have Skin in the Game
Unquestionably, talent is the most vital part of an organization's future. By committing to bringing in more diversified professionals, salaries in HR would have to be commensurate with those in other professional parts of the organization. The compensation structure should be directly related to the effectiveness of every function in the organization. As the talent development professional's chief responsibility is to recruit, hire, retain, and grow great workers, his or her pay and bonuses should be tied to the success of those workers. With linked compensation, imagine how differently talent professionals will act, how much more involved they would be in growing the business, nurturing the talent long-term and also, day to day, partnering with the talent to continuously improve and master risk-taking behaviors.

Step 4. Have Talent Leads Partner and Sit with Organizational Functions
This is the area where I see the greatest potential. Creating a team-like environment, where talent leads partner with and work in the trenches of the departments they hire for, will build closer relationships between areas. The talent lead's job is not to serve as Big Brother but more like the IDEO "mom" example I shared earlier. This person should associate and nourish at a highly engaged level

but also get into the nitty-gritty to make the unit function more seamlessly. For example, if a marketing director needs a Power-Point presentation by 5:00 pm and her deputy is out of the office, it is the job of the talent lead to find out who is available to help. By being a part of the team, the talent lead also will have greater knowledge of the strengths and weaknesses of the department, teams, and individual employees in real time and can work to fix ineffective processes and behaviors. By being in the trenches, the talent lead can enforce the culture, work to shepherd the innovation process described in the Improvisational Innovation chapter, and provide the team with a better feel for the culture and the communications practices that are helping or hurting business growth.

Step 5. Help Teams Network and Spot Opportunities
One of the reasons it is so hard to grow and develop talent is that organizations do not put enough emphasis on networking their people inside the organization. After spending time at a company that has about 30,000 employees, I realized that the young engineer I was helping shepherd his invention through the innovation process had no idea whom to turn to as mentors and partners outside of his immediate group. This engineer was working on a robotics innovation that involved three other divisions of the organization, and he didn't have a clue on how or whom to reach out to in these other groups. Why shouldn't this engineer have the opportunity to do a temporary detail in the division where his idea best fits?

Francine Parham, who held senior HR roles at both General Electric and Johnson & Johnson, realized that the lack of social networking within organizations impacted the bottom line. In response, she started a curriculum called "Maximizing Your Network" to focus on the science of social network systems, networking strategies, effective utilization of networking processes, and approaches to achieve desired outcomes. "It wasn't until I left my last role as a global VP of HR that I realized how limited my own network was. I had spent all this time directing people in HR roles but not nurturing my own network or the networks of those

I was leading," Parham said.[10] Since launching Maximizing Your Network, Parham has worked with corporations to build out their networking strategies. Networking within the organization is the key for helping people reach their maximum potential, she realizes. By networking employees across divisions, you not only give employees exposure to the larger organization, but the mentor/mentee role serves to edify both individuals—mentors often learn just as much from mentees as mentees learn from mentors.

The talent lead should keep anecdotal and documented information on what team members want to do next in order to increase the members' skill and knowledge levels so they have a better shot of being able to move toward their desired job. Just like ideas, if people are not nurtured, they stagnate. The talent lead should build a library of opportunities, potential projects, and temporary job-switching roles to serve as real-time and preparatory learning for talent development. It is the talent lead's job to help each individual team member get to the next stage of their career, even at the expense of possibly losing great talent to another division. As talent leads do so, they always must be on the hunt for the next generation of talent.

Step 6. To Ensure Passionate Employees, Value People and Help Solve Their Problems

According to the U.S. Bureau of Labor Statistics, in January 2012, employee tenure with their current employer was a mere 4.6 years.[11] Attrition is expensive and disruptive at every level. Consider the results from a November 12, 2007, survey titled "Employees Seek Better Information on Comp and Benefits," produced by CareerJournal.com, the executive career site of *The Wall Street Journal*. In the survey, HR professionals and managerial or executive employees cited the three top reasons they would begin searching for a new job: "53 percent seek better compensation and benefits. 35 percent cited dissatisfaction with potential career development. 32 percent said they were ready for a new experience."[12]

However, original research conducted for this book suggests that what also drives employees to seek out new opportunities is how they are treated. Many respondents feel totally devalued, using phrases such as "sweatshop," "treated like a dog," and "suck the life out of you."

How might a company value its people more and incentivize them to stay? The answer can be surprisingly simple. It may not sound revolutionary, but in the twenty-first century, if you treat people with dignity, recognize that we all face many of the same challenges as human beings, and nurture their interests, you may just get people to stick around longer.

Google was having issues with losing female employees after they gave birth. It surveyed employees to see how to solve the problem, and what bubbled up was a five-month maternity leave plan. According to a *Slate* article titled "The Happiness Machine: How Google Became Such a Great Place to Work," after the policy was in place, Google experienced an attrition rate among new mothers consistent with the average rate of other demographics. "A 50 percent reduction—it was enormous!" says Lazlo Bock, Google's head of people operations.[13]

Step 7. Strip Away Unnecessary Rules

Futurethink is a an innovation consulting and training firm that has developed an outside-of-the-box approach, what it calls "kill a stupid rule," that eliminates any rule that is not absolutely necessary to the function of that group. Team members come together and begin with the question "If you could get rid of any rule in the company—either kill it or change it—what would you do?" In almost any company that undergoes this exercise or something similar, people discuss where they find inefficiencies that leadership has not necessarily thought of. This exercise should be practiced within the HR function first, and then talent professionals should bring it to the groups they work with.

The other benefit to stripping away unnecessary rules, provided there is action after this exercise, is that non-HR professionals feel as if they are heard and are true partners with the talent lead in their group.

Identify Your Future STEM Workers Early, and Get Them in the Pipeline

When the Society for Human Resource Management (SHRM) conducted its annual Workplace Forecast Survey in 2013, no one was surprised to see the high cost of healthcare topping the list of greatest concerns. But for the first time, 68 percent of the companies surveyed ranked the lack of science, technology, engineering, and math (STEM) graduates as a factor that would have a "major impact" on the workplace over the next five years.[14] "The first problem here is that 86 percent of Americans don't know what the acronym STEM even means," says Julie Silard Kantor, chief partnership officer at STEMconnector, a Washington, DC, membership-based company focusing on STEM stakeholders.[15]

According to the Bureau of Labor Statistics, by 2020 there will be 9.2 million jobs in STEM.[16] Of those jobs, more than half— 4.6 million—will be in computing, compared to 2.8 million in engineering and 0.6 million in the life sciences. Computing will be one of the top ten fastest-growing job areas, with more than 150,000 new jobs opening every year, representing a 22 percent job growth rate. At the same time, between 1993 and 2008, the median age of scientists and engineers rose from 37 to 41, and domestic graduates cannot replenish the ranks quickly enough. As those statistics make clear, the economic well-being of the United States depends on computing, which in turn depends on a robust computing workforce. From 2011 through 2015, the shortfall of qualified computer scientists is expected to reach 51,000. In order to meet the demand, STEM grads will have to be brought in from outside the United States. According to a public radio segment, the United States graduates roughly 70,000 engineers per year, in comparison to China and India at 500,000 and 200,000 respectively.[17]

The need for STEM graduates is growing at a far faster rate than anyone expected, far beyond other traditional jobs.

In a report titled "Game Changers: Five Opportunities for US Growth and Renewal" by McKinsey & Co., if the United States wants to remain competitive, it

> must build a more cohesive and effective system of education and talent development in order to cultivate a productive workforce that can meet the challenges of a technology-driven global economy. . . . By taking action at both the K-12 and post-secondary levels, the United States could add between $165 billion and $265 billion to annual GDP by 2020. But even more striking effects would follow as better-educated students continue to filter into the workforce in the years ahead. This could produce a large "liftoff" effect, raising annual GDP by up to $1.7 trillion by 2030.[18]

Pierre Gauthier, CEO of Alstom, a leading energy solutions and transport company, states in the STEMconnector report "100 CEO Leaders in STEM," "We simply cannot preserve America's role as an epicenter of innovation, create new jobs and make our country more competitive on the global market without doubling-down on effort to train a more STEM-oriented workforce."[19]

Natarajan Chandrasekaran, chief executive officer and managing director of Tata Consultancy Services (TCS), a leading global IT solution and consulting firm, is a technopreneur who is known for making big bets on new technology. He is also deeply concerned about the future of human capital, specifically STEM education. "There is no doubt that a nation that is technologically savvy will inevitably have a competitive edge," Chandrasekaran says in the same STEMconnector report. "As we become more 'digital' as a society, not only does STEM education lead to technology-led innovations, but also increased competitiveness and productivity of a country."[20]

So, in 2009, Chandrasekaran decided to go big and launch goIT Student Technology Awareness Program, "a multi-tiered outreach program engaging students, parents, universities and local governments with the goal of increasing student excitement and participation in technology-related careers." The key ingredients of goIT include impact-based volunteerism, where TCS employees assist high school teachers on programming topics; job-skills gap assessment to identify the gap between postsecondary education and what the workplace needs; and summer camps that provide exposure to STEM jobs, role models, and technologies. "The program has evolved from a two-school camp to a national, year-long program that has influenced over 7,000 students across 35 school districts." According to goIT sources, in 2013, the program expanded to schools and students across 11 cities in the United States as well as Toronto, Canada. Throughout the summer camp, students were involved in a number of design, development, and implementation projects.[21]

Tom Jemison, a junior in college at Northern Kentucky University (NKU), first attended Tata's goIT Student Technology program in 2009, when he was 15 years old. Jemison first heard of the program at his high school. "I had just taken my first programming courses in school and was interested in IT at the time. . . . The ability to meet people who work in the industry locally was my biggest takeaway. It showed that I didn't just like computers but also enjoyed the people I would be working with if I continued learning about computers," he says.

Jemison maintained his interest in STEM subjects after the goIT program. He is currently a junior in college double majoring in computer science and information technology. He has interned with Tata two summers in a row and hopes for a third. From his experiences with STEM and exposure to software development, Jemison plans on joining a project to give NKU an in-house development team for gaming. "The program took me from being interested in IT, to knowing that I wanted to build my career around IT. The program made me feel like I had a company that was going to be interested in hiring me once I graduate from college, which is a relief," says Jemison.[22]

CHAPTER FIVE

Improvisational Innovation

Two Words That Will Turn Employee Ideas into Execution

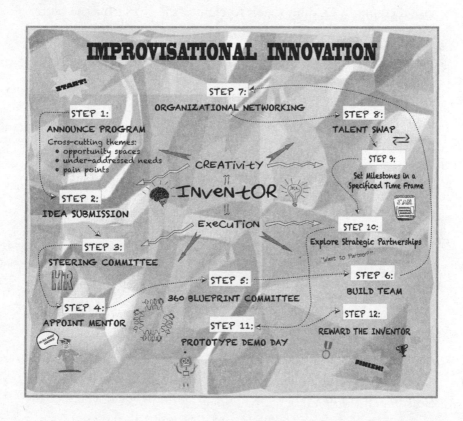

In a February 2014 interview with Dr. Paul Jacobs, then the CEO of the wireless technology company Qualcomm and now its executive chairman, it dawned on me that there were common threads among the world's leading innovators that no one had yet defined. First, it may sound trivial, but I found that most of these guys loved Legos as children and perhaps still do. (Larry Page is an AFOL [adult fan of Legos], and built the housing for the first Google server prototype out of Legos.) Second, they continue to roll up their sleeves and tinker, building gadgets and prototypes with their "buddies," as Jacobs said to me. Third, they admire each other and feel that they give each other license to dream bigger and even further out there. (When one thinks about colonizing Mars, the others are liberated to push the envelope.) Fourth, they all have a common guiding vision to change the world for the better. (Making money is a by-product, not the driving force.) Finally, as I mentioned in the Bold Character Leadership chapter, they think of themselves not as CEOs but as chief product or innovation officers and, in doing so, welcome great ideas from anyone at anytime—a methodology I call improvisational innovation.

Creativity + Accessibility + Execution =
Improvisational Innovation

NetApp's CEO said to me, "I am thrilled that we had a billion-dollar idea last year, but how do I know if there aren't 10 other billion-dollar ideas floating around in my employees' minds that I don't know about?"[1] Improvisational innovation solves that problem. From the employee perspective, what does someone do if they have a great idea? Whom do they turn to? If an innovative culture is nonexistent and/or a lack of trust exists, does the employee take the risk of sharing an idea with their own manager, who happens to be in a bad mood that day and squashes the idea? Or does the manager, who sees the value in the idea, opt to take credit for it herself?

While good ideas exist everywhere, what most organizations struggle with is a team that can effectively execute them. The methodology behind improvisational innovation can work for

> **Improvisational innovation** can be defined as engaging all the talents of your people, irrespective of job title, education level, pay grade, and so on. Like any good improviser, you are listening actively, you are open to change, and you develop a feeling for the right moment to act. Improvisational innovation creates a temporary space with no limits or rules to create barriers. It invites participants across the organization to be in the moment, generating anything from incremental to groundbreaking innovations (five to ten years down the road).

any organization, because it is accessible and a more pragmatic approach to building upon the assets a company currently has—driving smaller incremental steps while also increasing the chances of a major breakthrough. It focuses on accelerating ideas that advance the company and build a culture that is fast and adaptive without interrupting the bottom line. Because this type of innovation encourages creative pursuits, it just might keep your greatest talent from jumping ship. If an organization can make space for an entrepreneurial type to access the resources and rewards of a big company, chances are the organization will have less of an attrition issue. There are five factors behind the methodology of improvisational innovation. They are:

1. **Democratize the process so great ideas can bubble up from anyone at any time.** In Silicon Valley, there is an adopted belief that every person is responsible for the success and failure of an organization. The mind-set invites anyone to participate in the invention process. Currently innovators are defined and determined by the industry they are in, and therefore it is the *industry* that denies participation. In big pharmaceutical, for example, while innovation is market driven, scientists are the innovators. In software or SaaS (software as a service), the chief technology officer and the engineering

team are the innovators. In fashion, it is designers. You get the idea. The powerful difference in improvisational innovation is that inspiration can come from everyone, in every role, in every corner of the company. However, in order to effectively democratize the ideation process, there has to be an environment of optimism and humility when individuals share their ideas, so that each person feels encouraged to propel their idea forward.

2. **Adopt a formalized process that will enable execution on a specific timeline.** The innovator's idea needs to move from concept to prototype and beyond, with everyone thoroughly understanding what needs to be done and how long it will take. A formalized process allows time for experimentation, additional staff support, financial investment, and accelerated implementation, and adheres to a specific schedule that everyone is aware of. A suggested improvisational process and timeline can be found in the case study of Qualcomm's invention program at the end of the chapter.

3. **Ensure that the inventor has access to the right people at the right time.** A great idea needs an advocate who can strengthen an idea, shepherd it through the organization, get it to the right people at the right time, and be on the hunt for a group to potentially fund and prototype it. Additionally, the inventor should network with colleagues outside of the group they work in and even be detailed over to the business unit where the invention best fits in. For example, if an idea comes from a financial analyst (who is a robotics hobbyist), but the idea is positioned for a robotics system unit, the inventor should have the opportunity to network and do a temporary work detail in that unit so he or she gains a deeper understanding of how that unit operates and how the invention best fits in. This will ensure that all viable ideas on the table are not left unattended.

4. **Reward the inventor.** If someone has brought you a bold bet that results in significant revenue increase, a new revenue

stream or cost savings, leadership needs to recognize the inventor and his or her team, and reward them financially and otherwise. The inventor should receive special recognition, be known for the product invented, and have equity ownership in the product.

5. **Archive all ideas, good and not so good.** Ideas not viable today might just be perfect in the future. Lyn Heward, the former president and chief operating officer of Cirque du Soleil, describes how the company warehouses failed or unused show ideas, sometimes finding the perfect use for an idea a decade later. It also catalogs unique talent in every corner of the globe and uses this database as an inspiration for future shows. To continue with its mission to "constantly evoke the imagination, invoke the senses and provoke the emotions of people around the world," Cirque du Soleil has developed some of the most advanced processes to continue to enable groundbreaking innovation.[2]

THE BARRIERS IN INNOVATION TODAY

Most organizations are incapable of groundbreaking innovation for two reasons: (1) leadership does not engage the creative potential of the entire organization and its stakeholders; and (2) leadership cannot effectively execute due to ineffective organizational structures, insufficient leadership skills, and underengaged cultures that preclude people from experimenting. Ever since management guru Clayton Christensen's 1997 book *The Innovator's Dilemma* flew off bookshelves, the term "disruptive innovation" has been ridiculously overused and its very definition has been diluted.

The Disruptive Myth

Coined by Christensen, disruptive innovation is when "a product or service first takes root in simple applications at the bottom of a market and then relentlessly moves up market, eventually displacing already established competitors."[3] While this is the Holy Grail of innovation, it is incredibly rare to achieve. Very few companies, even the most buzzworthy start-ups, regularly achieve disruptive innovation. Why? First, disruptive innovation is not a strategy or a business model. Disruptions are often unpredictable, so there is no way to strategically prepare for them. A disruptive innovation often is something that happens randomly or by accident. Some of the best disruptive innovations happened by tapping into human nature, such as Apple's first graphical user interface (GUI), which was envisioned by Steve Jobs in regard to how he wanted to engage and work with a computer. Second, in the incumbent world, many leaders have remarked to me that when a person is striving for disruption, they inevitably face mental and emotional roadblocks because there are the wrong people in the wrong positions to execute an idea, and the company does little to incentivize an inventor to bring forth new ideas.

Furthermore, only a small group of companies change the future; the nature of economics dictates that everyone else has to follow. Often it takes a company that has a tremendous amount of cash on hand and accepts that they will have an exceedingly small batting average of success when experimenting with new inventions. They redefine failure as learning opportunities, incremental steps that get them further ahead of their competitors for the short—and possibly—long term. Regardless, the economy can't absorb continuous disruption, nor can consumer behaviors adapt to the changing pace.

Management Styles

As I argue in the Smart Work chapter, the very nature of work is changing. Whether you like it or not, the workforce is on the path to greater autonomy. If you are lucky enough to get to experiment in an innovative culture, chances are you actually are having "fun" at work, but for the vast majority of workers, their talents go unnoticed and the organization loses out.

Over the last five years, I have researched the barriers to and opportunities for innovation success at traditional companies, start-ups, and leading innovative companies that still maintain the start-up mentality. In doing so, I researched the dichotomy between organizations that have a steady flow of ideas but don't execute well and those that have the management ability to execute effectively but lack the kind of ideas that the world would embrace enthusiastically. Part of these findings include the greatest barrier to an organization's success: The management styles of a company's leaders determine what its company's innovations look like. Command and control hampers creativity, and free-flowing chaos is often challenged during execution. And further, often a misunderstanding of risk is what prevents companies from realizing their full potential.

SPECTRUM OF MANAGEMENT STYLES

Command and control	Free-flowing chaos
(incumbents)	(start-ups)

Neither extreme of management style is completely portable and/or appealing to the other: Command and control doesn't work in a start-up, and the start-up mind-set of free-flowing chaos will never take over the command and control world. However, there is a middle ground that strikes an appropriate balance for embracing innovative cultures. For most organizations steeped in a command and control hierarchy, pulling away would be a major cultural shift. However, hierarchy in an exponentially fast-paced world will kill innovation in any organization, so incumbent leaders are going to have to become more flexible to allow their people the freedom to experiment.

Conversely, a start-up can operate in chaos only for so long; then it gets too big and needs to put process in place, with the potential of losing the very people who made the start-up what it is in the first place. So, where's the sweet spot for innovative success? To find out, leaders must be willing to answer—honestly—three seminal questions:

1. Do you truly understand what innovation is for your own particular organization?
2. Do you understand how to innovate within your existing culture?
3. Do you understand how to motivate people who want to innovate beyond their day-to-day job?

At the moment, for most organizations, the answer to all three is likely no.

THE TRANSCENDENT WONDER OF INNOVATION

The key to innovation, according to Dave Blakely, an electrical engineer who heads up the technology strategy practice at the design and innovation consultancy firm IDEO, is to suspend disbelief and focus on opportunities and inspiration rather than on the risk. What is Blakely's definition of innovation? "Innovation is creation resulting from study and experimentation." Therefore, it is a learnable skill for anyone, not some innate talent of a chosen few. "Want to have a good idea?" Blakely asks. "Have a lot of ideas."[4] Indeed, companies that innovate best are those that have a myriad of ideas in process at once (recognizing that nearly all will ultimately fail), along with a process to propel ideas forward iteratively. But if just one becomes a commercial hit, the experimentation is worth it.

There are generally three ways for organizations to innovate: (1) insource: organic innovation (often the gold standard); (2) outsource: hire a creative services firm like IDEO; or (3) buy: acquire an innovative company. Blakely has observed that many successful companies do a blend of these three ingredients for rapid innovation.

The key is for the mix of approaches to be decided mindfully and strategically. Too many organizations, Blakely points out, devise an innovation strategy by happenstance.

Organic Innovation

Within organic innovation, organizations put money and energy into what they can do internally. More new innovation concepts and processes have sprouted over the past 20 years than in any other time in history. The most prevalent of these include: design thinking, disruptive innovation, agile/lean methods, and open innovation.

Design Thinking

Design thinking is anchored in the idea of human empathy, or "taking a walk in the user's shoes." The methodology, popularized by IDEO, imbues the full spectrum of innovation activities with a "human-centered" design ethos. Design thinking starts with a goal rather than a specific problem. For example, the Hasso Plattner Institute of Design (d.school) at Stanford University collaborated with JetBlue to identify a better customer experience. D.school design-thinkers hung out at airline terminals at San Francisco International Airport, observed human behavior for hours, and then began asking passengers open-ended questions, such as "What would make your terminal experience more comfortable?"

Bonny Simi, JetBlue's former director of airport planning, was able to bring design thinking to her work after she attended several d.school courses in 2006 and 2007. Simi was tasked with mitigating the dreaded "stranded on the tarmac for 11 hours" story that airlines were becoming increasingly infamous for due to circumstances, such as inclement weather, that were out of their control. She brought together all types of JetBlue employees, from pilots to bag handlers, to brainstorm unique ways they could better diagnose the problem while adhering to flight schedules. They

brainstormed from the perspectives of both crew members and passengers and came up with some groundbreaking ideas for navigating the gate and airport, disembarking from the plane, picking up
luggage, and finding ground transportation. Shortly after applying
the team's design-thinking outcomes, a 6-hour snowstorm in New
York caused a 24-hour shutdown at JFK airport. Typically JetBlue's
operations would have been impacted if not completely shut down
for about a week. This time the airline was able to get full operations up and running in a day. "I wouldn't have had the idea to
approach the problem in this way if I hadn't been to the d.school,"
Simi said.[5] "You realize that you aren't going to solve the problem
sitting in an office, you need to get out and talk to the people who
are actually dealing with it, whether that's your customers or your
frontline supervisors."[6]

Disruptive Innovation

As defined earlier, disruptive innovation capitalizes on emerging
market values and drives the growth of these values to the point
where established products and services become antiquated or
marginalized. Disruptive innovation is the most important innovation concept for game-changing risk-takers.

Agile/Lean Methods

Lean process production dates back to the fifteenth century with
the Venetian Arsenal, the state-owned, tightly clustered complex of
shipyards and armories, but it was Henry Ford who really popularized the concept when he married interchangeable parts with standard work and moving conveyance to create what he described as
"flow production," and which eventually became the assembly line.

Eric Reis, author of *The Lean Startup,* and Steve Blank, a
Silicon Valley serial entrepreneur, are most often credited with
reenergizing the movement. Lean methodologies measure ongoing results but then challenge processes as needed, as part of a

build-measure-learn loop. This is an important practice for great operational innovation. Agile methods, typically used in software development, help teams respond to unpredictability through incremental and iterative sprints, but lean methods work very well across the organizational structure. The iterative process reworks the scheduling strategy in products or processes by cutting out the deadweight and setting aside time to revise and improve any part of the system that is not at its leanest.

Open Innovation

Promoted by Henry Chesbrough, a professor at the University of California, Berkeley, open innovation describes "the use of purposive inflows and outflows of knowledge to accelerate innovation."[7] Simply put, firms can no longer rely solely on internal inventions to improve their products or processes but need to seek outside contributors in the process. The methodology behind open innovation has spawned new innovation platforms, such as idea competitions, crowdsourced collaborative networks, and customer-driven collaboration.

Improvisational Innovation

Improvisational innovation is today's important cultural component that answers every CEO's, CTO's, and chief innovation officer's question: What if my employees are walking around with the next big idea and I don't know about it? Improvisational innovation complements all other styles of innovation and builds an inclusive culture, where anyone and everyone can contribute ideas regardless of position, experience, education, and the like.

Improvisational innovation is a behavioral mind-set that:

- Supports the sharing of ideas without judgment.
- Develops superior listening skills by using the ideas of one person to trigger the ideas of another.

- Rides the wave of idea creation until the momentum slows or ends.
- Discards the limitations of the impossible.
- Engages impassioned discourse.
- Can happen at any moment, without preparation or a required result, unlike traditional planned brainstorming sessions.
- Allows a person to envision and create the job they want.

THE IMPERATIVE ELEMENTS OF IMPROVISATIONAL INNOVATION

In improvisational innovation, organizational leaders must think of employees as entrepreneurs and the company as the venture capitalist who can fund, partner, and commercialize a good idea. This is the starting point, and what follows is a string of six elements that need to be in place in order to effectively execute on an improvisational innovation process.

1. There must be an engaged, proactive commitment of the executive leadership, starting with the CEO. Ideally, the CEO has skin in the game and allocates funds to serve as a venture capital fund should a particular idea not get adopted into a specific business unit.
2. There must be an appropriate balance between risk-takers and more conservative members on an executive team so that every stone is turned and an improvisational innovation process is best positioned for success.
3. You must have entrepreneurial-type participants who are initially willing to explore and execute their ideas on their own time.
4. Once an idea is vetted and approved, you need to support the inventor fully and recognize that this idea has the potential to be the future of the organization.
5. If an idea is on the road to being commercialized, then you need to treat the inventor as a partner, offering a

predetermined amount of equity in the product or process that generates a new revenue stream.

6. Many ideas can be explored simultaneously with minimal investment. Improvisational innovation sets a pace for rapid prototyping.

Dynamic Behavior: A Culture of Fast Prototyping

While engineers are a vital part of improvisational innovation success, the way they are educated and trained is not conducive to rapid prototyping. Ideally, in the early stages of invention, broad aggregations of technology are considered and judgment is deferred. As the concept matures, typical "engineering thinking" should be employed, with a focus on feasibility, risk mitigation, and long-term reliability. "What we want to do is expand the modes of behaviors—over time—based on the phase of the project," says IDEO's Blakely.[8] After working with numerous engineers in various Fortune 500 companies, Blakely has discovered a problem in the way that engineers are taught to approach challenges. It is such an enormous problem that the solution to it could hold the key

DYNAMIC BEHAVIOR MAP

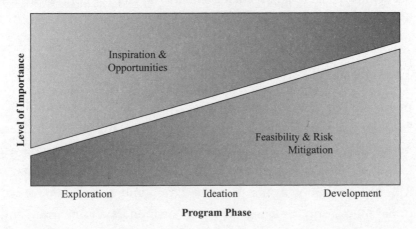

Inspiration & Opportunities

Feasibility & Risk Mitigation

Level of Importance

Exploration   Ideation   Development

Program Phase

to unleashing true internal innovation. He calls his solution "Dynamic Behavior," conveyed through three cycles in the innovation process: Exploration, Ideation, Development.

According to Blakely, most engineers spend 90 percent of their time in the Development phase, perfecting top-quality products and services with careful analysis, prototyping, modeling, and testing. By nature, many engineers are risk-averse people, and their training reinforces that innate conservatism. If you think about it, professionally, engineers are given a problem to solve by others and spend the majority of their time developing the solution based on a risk-mitigation paradigm of feasibility, budget, timeline, and safety factors. "Really, the engineer is taught to be heads-down, hold laser-focus vision on safe and reliable solutions, and crush deadlines," says Blakely. The nature of the discipline leaves little room for the Ideation or Exploration stages, when a team member might have a great idea to improve on existing technologies or envision the next disruptive experiment.

While working with a number of tech giants, Blakely has observed that engineers often provide correct and important information *but in the wrong context*. For example, during early explorations in the Ideation stage, an engineer who says something like, "Here's why your idea is too risky," probably means well, but the result is that ideation is shut down. Blakely asserts that all engineers must learn to adjust their behaviors to suit the context if they wish to play a role in innovation programs.

The Language of "Yes, and . . ."

In improvisational innovation, it is critical to set an optimistic, "anything is possible" mind-set and a vernacular that encourages, not squashes, people's enthusiasm for and comfort in sharing ideas. It is a poorly understood approach that most great leaders share. Like the well-known improv game "Yes, and . . . ," improvisational innovation combines creativity, awareness, momentum, and support, all with a goal in mind. It starts with an idea, and each successive thought begins with "Yes, and . . ." to build on the foundation. Such a brainstorming session might sound like this:

> Mitch: For the launch of our new product line, I want to throw a party.
> Terry: Yes, and we can make it a themed event.
> Mitch: Yes, and it can be something like a circus.
> Terry: Yes, and we can get one of those big tents with colorful flags.
> Mitch: Yes, and we can bring in clowns and pony rides for the kids.
> Terry: Yes, and we can have hot dogs and cotton candy.
> And so on.

This is not just an exercise in semantics. A culture that uses "No" during the ideation stage cuts ideas off, shuts them down, and often wounds people in the process. Even more prevalent is the culture of "Yes, but . . . ," which attaches judgments and conditions on an idea, limiting the possibilities. In both cases, these behaviors inadvertently discourage future participation. "Yes, and . . ." doesn't mean that all ideas will prevail in first ideation or at all, but people will be more likely to risk sharing ideas or contributing in creative ways if they are not discouraged.

"Yes, and . . ." is a liberating practice that invites the spontaneous free exchange of ideas. It is also a key to great risk-taking.

THE RISK FACTOR

My quest for the leading example of how improvisational innovation can work led me to an entrepreneurial culture that everyone is going to want to learn from: Qualcomm, a San Diego–based global leader in third-generation, fourth-generation, and next-generation wireless technologies.

Never Leave an Idea on the Table

On January 13, 2014, Navrina Singh, a mechanical engineer, stood at the front of a conference room on Qualcomm's campus to welcome 20 or so employee "inventors" to one-on-one design-thinking consultations with IDEO. Singh leads Qualcomm's formal invention program and, in my opinion, is the secret sauce to creating a motivated and innovative culture.

The program was the brainchild of Dr. Paul Jacobs, who happens to be the son of Qualcomm's founder, Dr. Irwin Jacobs. The younger Jacobs, who led the company as CEO from 2005 to 2014, always believed that great ideas could come from anyone at any level at any time, so he looked for a way to jettison the hierarchy and ensure, as Singh puts it, that they "have a visible voice for their ideas in Qualcomm." "There isn't a single silver bullet for innovation. At the foundation is a diverse, committed and passionate collection of smart people who don't accept conventional wisdom, but rather question assumptions and have the flexibility to take risks that turn ideas into the seeds of tomorrow's success," says Jacobs.[9]

Prior to the program's inception, Singh distinctly remembers the day she was called up to see Jacobs. Peggy Johnson, executive vice president of Qualcomm Technologies and president of global market development, and Matt Grob, executive vice president of Qualcomm Technologies and CTO, were also in attendance. Jacobs asked Singh, "Are you happy here?" Singh gave an emphatic affirmation. Jacobs responded, "Because happy employees create magic."

The three executives then asked Singh if she would be interested in running a new approach to an earlier program called the Qualcomm Innovation Network (QIN). QIN offered a business plan competition and engaged employees worldwide. However, it was time for QIN's evolution, based on changing needs of the business, market, and talent. Jacobs had four objectives in mind for the new program: (1) discover opportunities with breakthrough potential (new business initiatives); (2) develop corporate entrepreneurial leaders; (3) promote an entrepreneurial and innovation culture; and (4) explore and implement the "future of management principles," radical principles that suggest that everyone is responsible for innovation and should become a part of every company's "management DNA" (this is a phrase that Gary Hamel, a management guru, coined in his book *The Future of Management*).[10] To ensure the program's success, Jacobs created an innovation fund to finance prototypes for the ideas that were deemed worthy.

Johnson and Grob showed Singh a slide deck with four imperatives for the program: (1) make it technology focused; (2) incorporate experts; (3) make engineering talent the leads; and (4) have it look like something different from QIN—in other words, forgo the business plans that were required with the QIN program. Though the job still was largely undefined, Singh had a mandate to run it with a team of five. As she explored what the program would become, Singh was also tasked with thinking about other ways to build a stronger peer-to-peer community.

Singh spent the next four months meeting with executives to share Jacobs's vision and solicit their input on how the new program would function in their business units. She was planning to roll out a small pilot program when she ran into Joan Waltman (a former Qualcomm executive back to do some consulting) in the hallway. Waltman gave Singh two pieces of advice that somewhat contradicted one another: "Don't pull the yarn too quickly . . . let it unfold," and "You have to go global with your plan." In that moment, Singh knew that she needed Waltman to serve as a key advisor to the program. She recruited a few other internal Qualcomm employees and, after a grueling vetting process, told her new hires, "By the way, if you are not successful, this team may not exist next year." The innovation program started to take shape, with a marketing and program manager, an IT operations manager, and a technology lead to help inventors prototype their ideas. Collectively, the team created a formal program that would enable the ideas of any employee, irrespective of his or her job title, to bubble up and compete for prototyping and commercialization.

Singh believes that part of the magic behind Qualcomm's innovative culture is hiring the right kind of motivated talent, people who enjoy what they do day to day but also harbor enough curiosity to act beyond the immediate. For the process to work, Singh realized that the program needed three foundational elements: a safe and trusted environment, time, and resources.

The invention teams that succeed past the silent auction phase would be allocated 20 percent time (up to a day a week) for three months and a team of up to five other Qualcomm employees to work on the prototype. Singh also emphasized the importance of providing the right resources at the right time and allowing people to envision the job they want and to move on it. "Providing that right framework so everyone feels that their ideas are getting the right kind of attention is pivotal to engagement and finding the next big idea," Singh told me.

In order to help Qualcomm teams inspire, imagine, and evaluate new products and services, the program team focused on several important domains, such as the Internet of Everything, Pervasive Computing, Data Demand, and a category called Horizons, projects that look out five to ten years.

The first invention to be commercialized is the Internet of Things Development Kit, invented by a Qualcomm business development manager. The idea came to him while he was watching a YouTube video on using a phone to control an Arduino board, a single-board microcontroller intended for those interested in creating interactive objects or environments. According to the Internet of Things Development Kit description: "Developers want to create devices that interact with smartphones, but it's difficult, and while there are a myriad of options, there is no standard approach for connecting devices to phones. In this context, Things are consumer electronics devices or appliances, which work primarily in conjunction with a smartphone app, such as a connected thermometers and pedometers."[11]

Case Study: Qualcomm's Invention Program

This section explains how the Qualcomm invention program works. The program consists of three basic phases—Ideation, Review, and Prototyping—spanning about nine months.

Three Basic Phases

The Ideation phase starts with an official launch event at which the elements are announced. The elements are strategic areas of interest for Qualcomm, with many subthemes that provide a broad array of topics for brainstorming and ideation. Before a person submits an idea, the team recommends that he or she read through the content associated with each element on the internal Qualcomm website. At any time, employees can submit ideas for one or multiple elements. The program encourages employees to collaborate and connect with peers and experts by commenting and giving feedback on the website, as doing so may trigger new thinking and improve the overall quality of ideas.

In the Review phase, ideas submitted to the team are reviewed by subject matter experts (SMEs), selected based on their expertise and drawn from different divisions and functional areas across the company. Each idea will be reviewed by multiple SMEs to assess its potential. If an idea is not selected to move forward, the submitter can access feedback from the SMEs via the website. The goal of the team is to make the selection process and feedback transparent to the submitter.

If ideas are selected to move forward, they are graduated to the Silent Auction, during which time submitters showcase their ideas to sponsors, who have the option to bid on ideas. There are three possible outcomes from this stage:

1. A sponsor could recommend that an idea move forward into the Prototyping phase. Sponsoring may entail providing resources, mentoring, and/or providing guidance during the Prototyping phase.

2. If the idea aligns very closely with work being done in a business unit, it might be picked up by a sponsor of that business unit at this stage. In this case, the idea exits the invention framework and moves into the business unit. In this scenario, the innovation team will work with the idea submitter and the sponsoring business unit to ensure a smooth transition of the idea into the business unit. The idea submitter will have access to an innovation fund, providing financial resources to develop the idea further, and will get the opportunity to showcase the prototype/concept to sponsors and the managing board during the Executive Demo.

3. If the idea is not picked up by a sponsor and not recommended to move forward in the inventor framework, it exits the program at this stage and is archived in the system.

In the Prototyping phase, ideas that make it through the Silent Auction are prototyped over a period of three months. During this time, the submitters get some time to work on the inventor's projects and Qualcomm provides microfunding to transform ideas into tangible prototypes. This phase ends with the Executive Demo, where the submitter and team demonstrate the prototype or concept to executive sponsors.

Weekend Hackathons

In addition to the annual idea submission process, Qualcomm hosts employee hackathons, focused on company technologies, in multiple locations worldwide. The hackathon format provides internal customers' insights to help position Qualcomm products and technologies for success in the marketplace. The format allows for submission, refinement, review, and execution of ideas in a compressed invention weekend where concepts can be developed into working prototypes in as little as 30 hours.

Internal Lab or Dojo

Internal labs are great because they can identify a problem and pose the question "How do we solve it?"

Dojo is a Japanese term that literally means "place of the way." Earlier dojos were known as homebrew clubs. (The Homebrew Computer Club in the auditorium of the Stanford Linear Accelerator Center is associated with the launch of the Apple-1 prototype computer back in 1976.[12]) In Silicon Valley, a dojo is defined as a do-ocracy where people come together based on shared interests and passions, such as coding and robotics.[13] Hacker Dojo, for example, opened its doors in Mountain View, California, in 2009 and became the launch pad for many successful start-ups, including Pinterest.

David Crawley, a semiconductor physicist and founder of Hacker Dojo Robotics, shared with me that it had been a passion of his to pull robotics hobbyists together with 12 challenges in mind: drive around three cones, deliver a pizza from the front door of the dojo to a predetermined location inside, detect the face/ body of the owner, follow a predetermined target shape, follow a detected person to deliver a cooler of beer, identify a bad guy in a lineup, and draw a chess board outdoors with washable chalk, to name a few.[14] What Crawley built is a valuable case study of what any organization can easily replicate.

He learned quickly that many other people wanted to build robots in their free time as well. "What kind of people could we recruit if we created a self-selecting group who showed up for no reason other than because they loved building robots too?" he wondered. There was no pay, no incentives, no promise of anything, just people who liked building things as much as Crawley did. What he found, to his surprise, was that some of the people were exceptionally talented.[15]

Thirty people showed up for a single event after someone put the group on meetup.org, then suddenly Crawley found himself trying to run a group with more than 100 widely different people, such as a five-year-old who convinced his mother that he had to go, a CEO of a robotics company, a guy with a PhD who used to work for NASA, an imaging sciences PhD from Google, and a retired Lockheed Martin satellite engineer.

The group was intended to be self-managing, made up of individuals who were supposed to set their own hypotheses. Crawley deliberately was trying to provide only a minimum of technical help to encourage people to learn from each other and to self-select for people who could be self-learners. With more than 100 contributors, though, he needed to create some structure to partition and frame problems. Crawley created five cross-cutting themes and got the most technically capable people to form groups around each of the five themes.

Crawley and the other hobbyists then broke the problem down into small chunks, with each chunk intended to be something one person could do alone. In the spirit of Montessori learning methods, Crawley created a project box containing everything someone who wanted to learn about that part of the problem needed. For example, some of the boxes contained sets of electronic components, a robot architecture diagram, and a circuit board; other boxes contained a small computer. The goal was that anyone with technical competence could come in, take a box, make a meaningful contribution to the project, then put the box away at the end of the day and feel good about having built something cool.

Crawley's Hacker Dojo Robotics attracted exceptionally talented technical people; however, most were either not interested or not capable of swaying people in a particular direction. The farther away he removed himself from new recruits who joined the group, the less they tended to return. Crawley hadn't inculcated the vision of what he was trying to do deeply enough in the people who should have been driving these groups.

Another early mistake, Crawley admits, was not respecting people's ideas. He found that if you were even a little hard on a contributor's idea, he or she was unlikely to return. After all, you weren't paying them. If people couldn't make sense of the technical problem or stopped enjoying it, they generally peeled away. People who offer up their ideas are vulnerable. An idea by itself cannot be defended, but ideas are vital to the process, so they should not be denigrated. Respecting ideas paid dividends.

Later in the project an engineer came up with an idea for robots to navigate by sensors responding to ceiling lights. His assembly consisted of a few photodiodes in some blacked-out plastic bottles. Crawley took one look and thought, "This is clearly never going to work." He took a deep breath and then thought, "Well, how do I know for sure?" Rather than criticize the guy, Crawley responded, "That looks interesting . . . where do we go next?" The hobbyist dumped the plastic bottle photodiode idea pretty fast but went on to build a spectacular system, according to Crawley, that was able to determine the position of the robot within a few millimeters by looking at ceiling lights with a web cam. Crawley is convinced that this engineer never would have gotten there if his first idea had been squashed.

Key Lessons from Crawley
1. Self-selecting people around a compelling vision will always yield better results than recruitment to a prepackaged course that offers the same findings.
2. Respecting people's ideas means not denigrating them. Requiring them to prove the worth of their ideas will be infinitely more successful than a knee-jerk response.
3. The scientific method remains one of the best ways to close a learning problem, and everything is a learning problem.
4. Exceptionally talented people will not tolerate working with less than exceptionally talented people and will leave if it isn't worth their while.
5. People who don't contribute to the project are a drag on it. About 90 percent of the people are going to slow you down; 10 percent will move you forward.

CHAPTER SIX

Intellectual Property

*The Importance of Protecting Inventions and
a Parallel Intangible Asset Economy*

On January 13, 2014, Google made the stunning public announcement that it had acquired Nest Labs (Nest), a revolutionary home and business automation company, for $3.2 billion. The price tag was perplexing. Nest, cofounded by former Apple engineers Tony Fadell and Matt Rogers in 2010, only had—at most—$300 million in annual revenue. Most people around Silicon Valley were scratching their heads, wondering why the enormous acquisition price. Was it a technology play, with an eye toward expanding home automation, or a talent buy based on Fadell's and Rogers's stellar reputations? The answer will surprise you.

Intellectual Ventures (IV), a firm that partners with a network of inventors and creates, buys, and/or licenses patents, started working with Nest in September 2013. Nest entered into a deal to purchase patents from IV and to gain access, for defensive purposes, to the company's portfolio of over 40,000 patents. At the time, Nest was deeply embroiled in a patent lawsuit brought in February 2012 by Honeywell International, a global leader in energy efficiency products, and the IV deal was seen as a possible strategy for Nest to defend itself in that suit. Richard Lutton, Nest's chief intellectual property (IP) counsel, who worked with Fadell and Rogers at Apple, explains that the strategic move had broader implications: "For new, innovative, disruptive companies who are just starting the process of getting a foothold in terms of IP protection, it is important to partner and team with firms [such as IV] and to purchase intellectual property, to close any gap between innovation and the intellectual property required to protect that innovation in the marketplace."[1]

By January 2014, Nest had been granted 40 patents, which is quite a feat, given that it often takes two to three years to get a patent issued from the United States Patent and Trademark Office (USPTO). Through the deal with IV, it acquired 60 more and filed an additional 200 patent applications. Though revenue was not high enough to justify a $3.2 billion acquisition, in Silicon Valley, acquisitions can be based as much on talent and other assets as they are on current revenue streams. Sometimes companies with no revenue at all are bought for large sums—completely counterintuitive moves in the traditional business model. In this case, commentators have suggested that the price may have had to do with Google's desire to expand and grow its own IP in the complementary market provided by Nest and to give Google protection as it expands beyond Internet search and mobile.

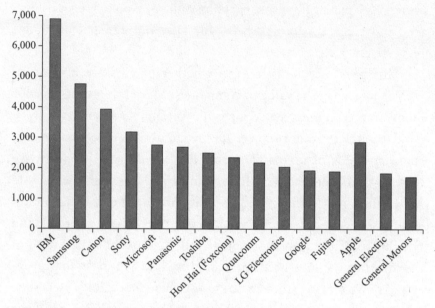

IBM TOPS U.S. PATENT RANKING FOR TWENTY-FIRST
CONSECUTIVE YEAR:
TOP 15 RECIPIENTS OF U.S. PATENTS IN 2013

Source: Information for Industry (IFI, USPTO)

Google's Nest Labs acquisition follows other IP-led purchases, most notably its acquisition of Motorola in 2012 for $12.5 billion. The Motorola acquisition took Google from a relatively weak patent position to boasting one of the largest cell phone patent portfolios in the country.[2]

That acquisition came on the heels of Google losing a bid for the Nortel patent portfolio. Google had bid $900 million, losing out to a consortium of companies comprised of Apple, Microsoft, RIM, EMC, Ericsson, and Sony. After a four-day bankruptcy auction involving not only the consortium and Google but also Intel and RPX, the consortium purchased the portfolio for $4.5 billion.

By acquiring Motorola and its patents, Google's patent issue rate was bolstered by 170 percent, catapulting the company to number 21 on 2012's list of top 50 patent holders, with 1,151 patents issued that year. This made Google the fastest-growing company on the list. In 2013, Google finally cracked the top 15 with 1,851 patent filings, surpassing Fujitsu, Apple, General Electric, and General Motors by 45, 76, 112, and 225 patent filings, respectively.[3]

This begs the question as to whether patents are playing an increasing role in the value of companies. More important, has our innovation economy created a parallel intangible-asset economy?

Although the innovation economy has always relied on the purchase and sale of intangible assets like intellectual property, we tend to think more often of companies and products being sold rather than the patentable ideas that support them. In an intangible asset economy, what is being incentivized and rewarded (and bought, sold, and traded) is not the full lucrative manifestation of the idea but the idea itself, protected by law as intellectual property. Are we moving from an economy where intangible assets such as IP merely protect the tangible assets to one where they have gained such disproportionally high value that they have formed their own parallel economy?

Traditional definition of intellectual property	Ideas, inventions, or creations protected by patents, trademarks, copyrights, and trade secrets.
Risk-taker's definition of intellectual property	A guarantee for inventors and their financial backers that hard work, time, and funds invested in the creation of something new will be rewarded if the new product/ technology finds a market; the intangible but no-less-valuable product produced by R&D that can be licensed, bought, or sold.

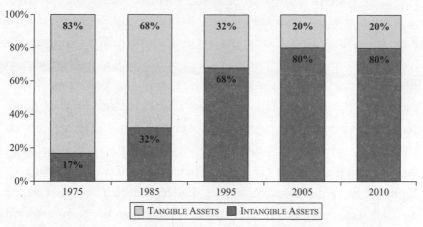

COMPONENTS OF S&P 500 MARKET VALUE

Source: Green Times

THE MARKET VALUE OF INTANGIBLE ASSETS

Let's consider what the data is telling us. One study by Ocean Tomo, an IP merchant bank, broke down components of Standard & Poor's 500 market value into tangible and intangible assets. The study concluded that intangible assets like IP comprise the largest U.S. asset class with a market value of approximately $5 trillion and with $1 trillion invested annually in the United States.[4] The study demonstrated that, over a 30-year period, the percentage of market value attributable to intangible assets has grown from 17 to 80 percent.

Investment in intangible assets has also increased. One study shows that the average investment rate in intangible assets from of 1948 to 2007 was 8.6 percent (compared to 11.4 percent for tangible assets). For the more recent period from 1995 to 2007, the average rate was up to 12.8 percent (compared to 10.4 percent for tangible assets). The ratio of intangible to tangible asset investment has gone from 3:4 to 5:4.[5]

Is this trend unexpected? Over the last several centuries, the secondary market for patents has ebbed and flowed, consistently surging during periods of significant technological advancements.

In the United States, as early as the nineteenth century, patent and copyright systems were press headliners with stories about negative-sum "patent wars" that were waged in boardrooms (culminating in huge litigation costs). Earlier claims and counterclaims were established when the British Statute of Monopolies authorized the world's first statutory patent institution in 1624, enduring centuries of sporadic growth. In 1950, economists Fritz Machlup and Edith Penrose published an article on patent controversy to prove that "despite all the changes in the economic scene, our thinking on the subject has hardly changed over the century."[6] They described the historical evolution of the patent system and its tendency to generate discontent and debates, culminating in a call to abolish patents in the second half of the nineteenth century.[7] In "Trolls and Other Patent Inventions: Economic History and the Patent Controversy in the Twenty-First Century," Zorina Kahn, an economist and historian, says that "facile rejoinders to historical accounts tend to dismiss such experiences as irrelevant to the twenty-first century and the Brave New World of smartphones, silicon chips, and one-click patents."[8]

Let's take another look at Google's acquisition of Motorola. Other than the fact that Google itself confirmed that the purchase was motivated by Motorola's patents, how can we tell that patents played such a large role? For one thing, Google sold Motorola in two years for a fraction of the cost. Google purchased Motorola and its patents in 2012 for $12.5 billion, retained a majority of the Motorola patents, then sold off the company, along with 2,000 Motorola patents and a license for the rest, to Lenovo for $2.91 billion. It doesn't take a lot to do the math on this one (and even the sale to Lenovo was, in large part, a patent play).

Not only are patents an important component of a company's value proposition, but, as the Nest case illustrates, it has become increasingly important that a company's innovation not outpace its investment in IP.

Nest's story is not unique. Facebook found itself in a major legal battle with Yahoo! in March 2012 as it was getting ready for its initial public offering (IPO), and its meager 56 patents weren't enough to defend it in the social media space. Not only had Facebook's investment in innovation and its resultant growth far exceeded its investment in intangible assets like IP, but over 90 percent of Facebook's patent applications were still pending. What did Facebook do? Something that has become commonplace with the advent of rich, secondary markets for patents: It bought its way out. In March 2012, in what was not their first acquisition of patents, Facebook paid an undisclosed amount to purchase 750 patents from IBM, even countersuing Yahoo! on some of those patents. Facebook later paid $550 million to buy 650 AOL patents from Microsoft, which had acquired them as part of a $1.1 billion deal earlier in the year.

Even if Facebook had invested significantly more resources into developing its homegrown IP, its rate of innovation was outpacing its development of intangible assets. It can take years to secure a patent, and as most of today's technologies build on past technologies, any attempt to rely only on homegrown IP would be riddled with land mines. Generally speaking, the only way a young company can be fully protected both offensively and defensively is to purchase patents that predate its own existence or to reach a licensing deal with the owners of earlier patents. For example, ElliptiGO created a great new kind of bicycle that's easy on the joints and is licensing technology from the creators of the elliptical to do so. In other words, one technology, shared through the patent system, helped give birth to another. In today's cell phone industry, the landscape is no different. Cross-licensing or licensing deals involve almost every player and contribute significantly to technological evolution.

The desirability of patents both as an asset category and as a tool to shore up IP to match the pace of innovation can be seen in patents sales over a recent three-year period. According to Ocean Tomo, from 2011 to 2013, there have been consistent sales of patent portfolios of 250 patents or more. These sales include, in addition to the Nortel sale, 2011's sale of 1,914 patents from Mitsubishi to Renesas Electronics, 2012's sale of 1,700 patents from Interdigital to Intel, and 2013's sale of 900 patents from IBM to up-and-coming Twitter.

HOW CAN IP INCENTIVIZE INNOVATION?

It is clear that there has been a shift in value from the tangible to the intangible. Innovation is not just being protected by patents and IP; today patents and IP are themselves seen as innovations that can be independently monetized. In this model, we are left to ask: How do we incentivize intangible "innovation"?

The risk/reward model for intangible assets is much more nuanced and risk focused than for hard assets. An inventor's intangible innovation success rate should be thought of like a baseball batting average. Even for the best inventors (like the best ball players), the hit rate is low. Even IV's Nathan Myhrvold, one of the company's founders and the former chief technology officer of Microsoft, who is widely noted as a visionary technology and business leader, estimates that his "batting average" for innovation is only 40 percent.[9]

To properly incentivize the creation of new inventions, one needs to provide an appropriate upside to each player to counterbalance the shockingly high risks. Just as venture capital firms and other industries arose to enable the creation of start-up companies, intangible assets will be funded though a similar model. An entire economic ecosystem is growing to incentivize and reward invention. As with any market, new funding sources and strategies are being created to aggregate ideas and risks to provide diversification. And, as with any market, there are inefficiencies as we try to find ways to manage undesirable secondary risks.

Let's step back.

When people think of the law, they usually think of a set of rules and a corresponding system designed to minimize risk and/or to shift the costs affiliated with those risks to the person most responsible or best able to bear those costs. Most of us have internalized, for the most part, the "rules" or "laws" that apply to us. We don't necessarily think of our behavior as governed by those laws until we experience an event or circumstance that causes us to question or invoke those laws.

Patent laws, however, differ. Unlike most of our laws, they are not meant to discourage risk but rather to *encourage* risk.

Beginning with the 1624 Statute of Monopolies in England, patent laws were put in place to encourage risk-taking and innovation by rewarding inventors with a limited monopoly over their inventions. These concepts were later adopted by the United States in Article 1, Section 8, Clause 8 of the U.S. Constitution: Congress shall have power "to promote the progress of science and useful arts, by securing for limited times to authors and inventors the exclusive right to their respective writings and discoveries."

Congress has exercised this power by granting to inventors 20 years of exclusivity for their inventions in exchange for inventors fully disclosing their inventions to the public and enabling the public to make and use (under license or after the patent expires) of them. During this period of exclusivity, others cannot make, use, offer for sale in the United States, or import into the country the invention without the permission of the patent holder. This "monopoly" was designed to incentivize individuals to invest human and fiscal capital in research and development.

But some critics of the patent system say it is broken and that patent laws encumber, rather than encourage, innovation. They believe that there are so many potential patents that might cover future innovation that the patent minefield is virtually impossible to navigate when one wishes to develop something new. By way of example, RPX (a provider of patent risk management services) estimates that there are approximately 250,000 active patents that cover smartphones.

Yet this criticism is based only on theory. To turn RPX's example around, the consumer cost of smartphones over time has become more affordable both in rich countries and in the developing world, while competition in the handset industry thrives. Apple was able to usurp Nokia's crown as industry leader almost overnight thanks to the iPhone, only to see Samsung vie for that title just a few years later—even as HTC and any number of other competitors jostle for the consumer's attention. While Apple and Samsung have clashed over patents in high-profile patent litigation—a conflict with such outsized financial rewards at stake it seems to exaggerate the scale of patent litigation as a whole—the patents they dispute mostly cover the form and surface functionality that set their products apart from each other.

What their products and nearly every other smartphone share is the connectivity technology that allows one caller in Los Angeles to seamlessly speak with another in Beijing and a third in Prague, even as all three of their devices receive and send email, stream video, and handle what seems like an infinite number of business and lifestyle tasks.

Qualcomm, one of the principal companies responsible for making that connectivity possible, says it was able make the technological breakthroughs thanks to the patent system. When the seven founders of Qualcomm first gathered in a San Diego living room, they knew they wanted to solve technological problems that were holding back wireless communications, but they didn't have a product.[10] They originally had in mind invention and innovation, rather than production. Instead of a product, they had ideas—ideas that kicked off years of research and development. The result was technology that vastly expanded how many calls cellular networks could handle at once and eventually enabled them to carry data.

But such R&D is risky, expensive, and lengthy. Qualcomm was able to take the risks because the patents on its early ideas were strong enough to persuade financial backers to give the company a chance. Once Qualcomm succeeded, it licensed its technologies to companies throughout the industry and plowed the licensing revenue back into R&D, creating what Qualcomm now likes to call a virtuous cycle of innovation: R&D producing new technologies, which are licensed to the makers of handsets and other wireless devices, producing revenue that in turn funds more R&D that creates newer technologies. By the end of 2013, Qualcomm had spent $27.3 billion on such innovation since it opened shop in 1985. And the massive wall of patents greeting visitors (photo at the beginning of the chapter) at its San Diego headquarters is a testament to how much it reveres, relies on, and credits patents for its ability to innovate.

A DECADE AND MORE OF VAST CHANGE

Kathi Lutton is an IP/patent litigator and strategist at the law firm Fish & Richardson, a leading IP firm that has represented Thomas Edison, Alexander Graham Bell, and the Wright brothers. An electrical engineer who went to law school, she represents many of the world's most innovative companies, such as Apple, Hewlett-Packard, NVIDIA, SAP, and VMware. I asked her about how IP law and the incentive structure for risk have evolved in our society over the past 20 years.[11]

Lutton says that we have seen new business models evolve over the past 10 to 15 years that enable the intangible asset market and/or impact the risk/reward incentive structure. In terms of enabling the intangible asset market, business models have evolved to make the market for patents and IP more liquid. Lutton stated that Myhrvold once shared, "The fact is we all need a liquid invention market, where patents can be bought and sold for a fair market value. Inventors want to be paid for their work; companies of all sizes want to be able to make a return on their IP investment; and universities want to further research and development. Without this market, who will have the incentive to reinvest in invention, and in turn push ahead our collective economic growth?"[12]

One company that has been actively involved in building business models to improve liquidity in the intangible asset market is Ocean Tomo, which considers itself an IP bank that recognizes "Intellectual Capital Equity" as part of the broad definition of value. Ocean Tomo's first and most profound action was to create the first open, public market for the sale of patents and portfolios of patents. In 2006, Ocean Tomo held in San Francisco what it called the first live patent auction, drawing over 400 people, including many high-level IP professionals. Ocean Tomo sold a third of its patents for $8.5 million at that first auction and has been hosting auctions with even larger numbers ever since. In its first ten auctions, Ocean Tomo generated revenue of $114.6 million.

More recently, Ocean Tomo has developed a public exchange for patents. To facilitate the trading and purchasing of patents and to bring liquidity to the market, Ocean Tomo recognized the need for a system to quickly sort and evaluate patents. The company took a page from another non-homogeneous asset market, the mortgage market. For the mortgage market to obtain liquidity, it had to find a way to efficiently compare various borrowers. So it developed FICO, or credit scores, which assigned each unique individual a comparable metric. Ocean Tomo has developed a similar rating score for patents, the Ocean Tomo Ratings (OTR) score.

Ocean Tomo demonstrates that a more liquid market for IP has created greater rewards to incentivize innovation. As the liquidity of the market expands, so do patent filings. In 2009, there were 486,499 patents filed in the United States. The number has increased each year since. In 2013, filings were up to 609,052 (a 24 percent increase in only four years).

While Ocean Tomo was helping to create the market, IV entered with a new business model to further facilitate (or exploit, depending on your view) the market, creating what it calls the "invention capital market." IV has infused more than $2.3 billion into the economy since 2000, purchasing patents and fostering the market for invention and intangible assets.

Myhrvold, who had been exposed to patents in his former life at Microsoft, decided in 1999 to determine if he could use the patent system to spur innovation, not just in the abstract but in a laboratory in a suburb of Seattle. In August 2003, in what looks like an unassuming warehouse next to a boat storage and repair shop, Myhrvold hosted Invention Sessions, which continue today, bringing together some of most brilliant minds in the world, from Bill Gates to Ken Caldeira, a professor at Stanford working actively to solve global warming.[13] Myhrvold's friends gather around a large conference table and brainstorm new ideas in diverse areas, from solving the world's energy issues with new battery technology and less expensive nuclear plants, to how to predict hurricanes and de-liver vaccines to Africa.[14]

To date, IV has spun off three companies: TerraPower, which is working toward zero-emission energy, in 2008; Kymeta, founded to commercialize the metamaterial surface antenna, in 2012; and Evolv, which focuses on metamaterial-based security imaging, in 2013. Additionally, Global Good, a collaboration be-tween IV and Bill Gates, invents technology that improves life in developing countries.

When asked what the key was to his successes, Myhrvold stated that it was quite simple: "We are willing to take risks." And why is that? "Because the patent market provides sufficient rewards." As Myhrvold notes, in the not-too-distant past, we saw the rise of the venture capital market, NASDAQ, and the IPO market, all of which stimulated new companies and changed the world for the better. Yet all were quite controversial at the time, because they threatened ex-isting models and business. In Myhrvold's view, we are seeing the same evolution now with the market for intangible property:

> If we didn't have a lucrative market, we wouldn't be seeing the level of inventive activity we are seeing today. . . . Imagine if Mark Zuckerberg, founder and CEO of Facebook, was paid $100 a year. He would not have created what he created nor would others be trying to follow in his footsteps. What if an inventor is not good at doing a 9–5 job but wants to be a professor? What if he doesn't like people? What if she can't get a job at a glamorous start-up that offers free food, massages, and dry cleaning? We are that for them. We [IV] are investing in them and their great ideas. We are funding them. They are much more likely to continue to do more inventing if we assume the risks associated with invention.[15]

IV and Ocean Tomo are two of tens of companies that have evolved to change the intangible asset marketplace. Collectively, they are creating new incentives and are increasing patent filings and trading. Although we have seen much evolution in past years,

Jim Malackowski, the chairman and CEO of Ocean Tomo, notes that where we are today is just the beginning of a normal economic cycle.[16]

Public opinion of companies like IV and Ocean Tomo is split—many ongoing business concerns see the emergence of a secondary market for IP as a major threat, while others have invested in or teamed with IV in various ways. Regardless of where you fall in the debate, the reality is that the game is changing, and to thrive, you must take that change into consideration.

GLOBAL GROWTH IN INTANGIBLE ASSETS

In this chapter, I have focused on the U.S. economy, but the change in patent protection is global. According to Ocean Tomo, accounting practices throughout the world have evolved to reflect the fact that intangible assets are forming a more meaningful component of companies' value propositions. In 1970, U.S. Accounting Principles Board (APB) Statements 16 and 17 suggested accounting methods for dealing with intangible assets.[17] In 1983, the International Accounting Standards (IAS) discussed the accounting treatment for acquisitions of intangible assets through business combinations.[18] In 1997, the United Kingdom Accounting Standards Board allowed separately identified intangible assets *that could be valued* to be listed on a balance sheet.[19] (However, this practice is rarely used.) In 2001, U.S. Financial Accounting Standards (FAS) Board Statements 141/142 mandated acquired intangible accounting and testing for impairment, and IAS followed in 2005.[20] IAS 38.54 allows development costs for intangible assets to be recognized under strict criteria.[21] The 2010 German Accounting Law Modernization Act allows patents, optionally, to be shown on the balance sheet.[22]

In addition to accounting practices evolving to reflect changes in the economy, Ocean Tomo notes that measures worldwide also reflect the value assigned to IP.[23] In 2010, the Chinese government issued a policy for the use of patent rights for collateral in commercial loans. Twenty-four banks and 16 guarantee companies used

**U.S. IN-FORCE PATENTS, OCTOBER 2013,
WIPO STATISTICS DATABASE**

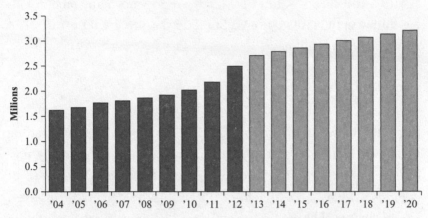

Source: Ocean Tomo, from WIPO Statistics Database; actual patents in force through 2012. Linear extrapolation for estimates for subsequent years.

IP as collateral for USD $3.7 billion. The Singaporean government encourages banks to use IP as collateral and includes governmental value guarantees. The Malaysian government also allocated USD $65 million for IP financing.[24]

Not only the United States is seeing increased growth in the number of patents in force. According to the World Intellectual Property Organization (WIPO), patent growth has increased in China, which once was very cold to patents. The SIPO, the Chinese IP authority, published a report titled "National Patent Development Strategy (2011–2020)," which states that one of the country's goals for 2015 is for China to rank among the top two in the world in terms of annual number of patents for inventions granted to the domestic applicants. They expect the annual quantity of applying for patents for inventions, utility models, and designs will reach 2 million.[25]

THE RISK FACTOR

Whether one agrees that our innovation economy has created a parallel intangible asset economy or not, one cannot ignore the significant impact, both positive and negative, patents are having on our economy and our incentive structures. In addition to her Fortune 100 clients, Kathi Lutton also represents many Silicon Valley and West Coast start-ups. She has the same advice for all of them, which I detail next.

Build Your Own IP

First and foremost, hire a top-notch IP strategist and start building your own IP from the ground up. Lutton cautions that many patent prosecutors (those who draft and file for patents on behalf of companies) have an end goal of obtaining the patents themselves. Lutton insists that goal is too narrow. She advises that you find a prosecutor (or patent team) that knows how to obtain and build portfolios that will meet all your needs, from protecting your products and protecting your market to business goals ranging from funding, licensing, marketing, and any potential exit strategies.

Lutton cites the example of a client who came to her with a patent that had been drafted by another law firm. The client needed a review to confirm that the patent was properly classified. Using an analogy to protect the client, Lutton recalls that the patent related to a method of combining two things, in much the same way as combining chocolate syrup and milk makes chocolate milk. But the patent was very narrow, suggesting only that the client owned a specific *way* of combining the milk and the chocolate, when in fact the client had invented the milk, the chocolate, the way of combining them, and the chocolate milk itself. The previous patent attorney was focused on the technological challenge (the way of combining), not on the end game. Of course, in the big picture, it is much more powerful to own the chocolate milk itself than the process that creates it.

Acquire or License IP

Lutton notes that there are two challenges for today's emerging companies. First, most companies are likely, in the words we attribute to Sir Isaac Newton but that he, ironically, borrowed from twelfth-century Bernard of Chartres, "sitting on the shoulders of giants." Most inventions today are, in the words of Peter Detkin, founder and vice chairman of IV, "evolutionary, not revolutionary." Every aspect of a smartphone is not new. Cameras are not new. Phones are not new. Music players are not new. In order to have a proper IP portfolio to cover new products, one needs IP that relates to every aspect of an invention (aspects inventors cannot possibly patent themselves, given the timing of their entry into the market).

The second challenge relates to timing in the Patent Office, as the average patent currently takes two and a half years to issue. (From 2008 to 2013, the average patent issue time ranged from a low of 29.1 months to a high of 35.3 months.) This means that it will take years for emerging companies to develop the IP they need to develop around their own innovation. And, if a company builds on the inventions of others, it can never catch up if it limits its IP strategy to developing its own IP. During the building time (and to cover inventions on which the company is building), it needs a stop-gap measure to avoid becoming an undefended target. One way is to acquire or license already-existing IP.

Enter into Strategic Business Deals with Patent Aggregators

Working with a patent aggregator is controversial in the eyes of many. Nonetheless, patent aggregators purchase patents and offer their customers licenses for those patents through various licensing models. In some instances, they purchase patents that are asserted against their customers in litigation to "buy" those customers out of litigation. Some companies see entering into strategic business deals with patent aggregators as a way to manage the risks associated with potential patent litigation. Others see the aggregators themselves as adding to the risks and costs.

Lutton has mixed views on the roles of patent aggregators, though some of her larger clients have benefited from these business models. She notes: "Some would say that patent aggregators take patents off the open market and out of the potential hands of companies who might assert the patents, and allow companies to pay a more reasonable price for protection for those patents and/or for the right to practice them. There are others who believe that patent aggregators themselves enable opportunistic behavior because they have found a way to scale and streamline patent assertion efforts."[26] Lutton has clients in both camps—and even some who believe the latter but still buy patent aggregation services to manage their risks.

As for advice, Lutton suggests fully understanding the risks and rewards of the aggregators and making decisions that best serve your company. She also notes that the decision of how and whether to partner with such companies needs to be continually revisited as their value proposition changes with the evolving law and marketplace (as well as, in some instances, the company's own changing model).

Carefully Consider Indemnity Issues (for Both Incoming and Outgoing Technology) and Insurance

When we talk about the risk and reward of the new patent economy, we can't ignore the classic risk-shifting models: indemnity and insurance. The concept of indemnity has become increasingly important as assertion entities sue up and down the value chain. Sometimes a smaller player gets sued because the assertion entity believes it is least able to defend itself. Sometimes the technology integrator (downstream supplier) gets sued because it has a larger revenue base. Depending on where a company sits within the food chain, it needs to decide whether to demand that suppliers indemnify it for any allegations of patent infringement and whether it wants to indemnify those to which it supplies product. And a company needs to consider what shape that indemnity takes.

Likewise, it would be wise to analyze whether to purchase insurance against patent assertions such as that offered by RPX.

The bottom line is that companies need to consider *all* the business options at their disposal, including indemnity and insurance, and to seek sound ongoing advice as new business models and offerings emerge.

Although the emerging marketplace may seem to present exciting opportunities, the world of patents isn't all roses. The market is still emerging and suffers from major market inefficiencies that impact clients. Today's more liquid patent marketplace has in some sense enabled younger companies to close the gap between innovation and patent protection, and it has also removed barriers to entry for companies to acquire patents and to challenge questionable patents. Many major companies are taking the lead in proposing legislation that will minimize inefficiencies, and despite enactment of the America Invents Act in 2011 (the most significant patent legislation in over 50 years) and recent changes in case law, there is much to be done to better protect inventors.

CHAPTER SEVEN

Smart Work

For thousands of years, people (with the aid of hand tools and animal power) worked without the benefit of power machinery. Craftsman and artisans often toiled through years of apprentice-ships, eventually becoming noted for the quality and uniqueness of their work. At the dawn of the industrial era, generally considered from about 1760 to sometime between 1820 and 1840, savvy risk-takers used advancements in modern machinery, transportation technologies, and mass-production management practices to scale up huge global companies capable of creating hundreds, even thousands, of products a day and shipping them to markets around the world. These companies were, in essence, huge machines.

To make machines work, you need each part to play a specific role, consistently and without interruption. In these first big enterprises, thousands of people made up the machine. Each role was defined, and each person was told to do their job within that specific definition—no more, no less. In actuality, each person was perceived to be a cog in a production that blended into the machinery. Today, over a century later, not much has changed. In fact, thinking about workers as cogs in the production wheel still is the prevailing model for today's organizations.

Yet those old rigid rules and strictly defined roles are chafing against the powerful speed of markets, which demand that companies become more innovative, agile, and valuable to customers. Companies are asking their workers to be more inventive and more effective while simultaneously still performing their traditional role in the machine. This clash of expectations is creating significant rifts within the organization.

What has caused the shift? As technology has evolved, so have people's expectations about all of life's opportunities—in the workplace, at home, and as consumers. We now have instant access to information, in real time. We can quickly reach our friends, family, or coworkers for trusted opinions and support. We can safely gain knowledge with controlled practice, virtual games, or live demos. Technology allows us to experiment, take risks, try different approaches, and experience more of what life has to offer.

We are also a more highly educated society than we were at the advent of the industrial era. According to the U.S. Census, in 1940, 35 percent of Americans 25 years and older had obtained a high school diploma or higher. By 2009, this number exceeded 80 percent, a number that remains consistent to this day.[1] How does this impact today's workforce? It means that we have three very different generations—Baby Boomers, Generation X, and Millennials—that all have grown up and been exposed to a wide range of technological advancements. Yet, because each generation has been introduced to the spectrum of technological advancements at different points, each generation has made a vast departure from the preceding one, momentously redefining their role at home and at work.

The culmination of contesting generations who don't necessarily see eye to eye on much of anything, and a smarter world that can access and manipulate information faster, calls for a dramatic overhaul of the workplace. We have been priming our workers with the tools and knowledge to take more risks for a long time. So why has the workplace itself failed to keep pace?

The personalization of consumer electronics over the last decade has been remarkable. Steve Jobs dreamed of a world where we would be walking around with handheld computers, and now we've got them. Google Glass goes a monumental step further as a wearable technology that communicates with the Internet via voice command. Technology has enabled us to work anywhere, yet most people still can't. Even at the office itself—unless you work at a tech company—tools and systems often are antiquated and inefficient and end up costing the company more money than if it had invested in technologies that offer simple solutions to complex problems. There is a dispiriting disconnect between the seamless personalization of consumer technologies and workplace offerings for employees.

IF NOT EMPLOYEES, MODERN TECHNOLOGY FOR CUSTOMERS?

Consumer-oriented industries have started to adapt better to customers' growing expectations. Take, for example, the car rental business. Hertz, Avis, Budget, Dollar, Enterprise, and National all have integrated time-saving technologies to bypass the rental counter so that you can get on your way much more efficiently. Hertz, for example, offers "Carfimation" as part of its Gold Plus Rewards program where a text message is sent directly to your phone with your rental car and its location—even your contract will be available in your rental car. It takes what was once considered an annoyance for the business traveler and makes it a fun guessing game to discover what kind of a rental car you are going to get.

But what if consumer-oriented industries were really thinking out of the box? Why not use technology to help us in the most convenient ways? A simple example is when we dine out. Although we are paying a premium to relax and not worry about preparing the food or cleaning up afterward, we are forced into awkward scenarios. As restaurant customers, we seemingly have to work harder to find great customer service. How often have you had to track down a waiter and, more often than not, feel as if you are a nuisance for asking for a clean fork or for requesting your check? As an alternative, why can't we be seated with a computer tablet on the dining table, where we can find out our waiter's name, view our ordering history, or press a button that calls our waiter over when something is not cooked right? Or, when we are ready to hustle out of there because we have to get on a conference call or need to whisk away three children on the verge of a meltdown, why can't tablets be available, so we can just pay the bill through a tablet or a mobile payment such as Square? All of this adds up to smarter, more efficient work that benefits the employee and the customer. Don't you agree?

Now, back to the workplace.

Traditional definition of smart work	While stationed in a sea of cubicles, your role is to take on as many projects as possible and spend tireless hours in order to prove to authority that you are worthy.
Risk-taker's definition of smart work	Redefining how, when, and where people work.

TO WORK IN THE OFFICE

Although I am an advocate for workplace mobility, which I discuss in great detail later, without a doubt there are industries and professions that need to be together in the office or under one roof. Those in creative endeavors or manufacturing, for example, benefit from being face-to-face. In some circumstances, it would be impossible to work remotely. No one has done the office lifestyle or the meshing of generations better than Google. In *Secrets of Silicon Valley,* I covered Google's unique work lifestyle, bringing the outdoors in and the work outside (should an employee decide to do some work outside at one of Google's pastoral campuses), offering healthy and organic foods, all for free, and well-being services such as on-site doctors, chiropractors, massages, workout facilities, swimming pools, renewal spots for on-site naps, and the like. Google's offerings go way beyond most people's imaginations; it has addressed almost any employee's personal concern from big, long-term issues, such as death benefits for your spouse, to those other little daily needs and nuisances, such as banking, dry cleaning, haircuts, oil changes, car washes, and bike repairs—all on-site at the Googleplex, the name of Google's headquarters. Google employees really never have to leave the Googleplex for anything.

Although the Googleplex has been around for over a decade and the ideas behind it are ripe for the replicating, I have yet to see many companies trying to accommodate the diversified workplace and the technological advantages in a similar vein. Google puts a premium on everything it takes to foster a creative and innovative environment. Play is embroiled into the life of Google, and I document the immense benefits of play at the end of this chapter.

Yes, Google owns a tremendous amount of square footage, 3.1 million square feet of space,[2] and a vast campus in Mountain View, California (in part because no Google building is higher than four stories).[3] Yet the company takes responsibility for its massive space and carbon footprint, generating much of its own power with solar-powered buildings, providing electric vehicles and bikes for employee use, and using employee shuttles powered by a fuel blend that has the lowest emissions. From a 360-degree perspective, Google epitomizes the definition of smart work in the workplace.

THE THIRD PLACE

Another aspect of smart work is maximizing commuting time on our highways—if we are going to have to continue to spend time commuting, we might as well get our commutes to work for us. While the national average of commutes is 25.5 minutes, according to the U.S. Census Bureau,[4] in metropolitan areas such as New York, Los Angeles, and Washington, DC, driving commutes have become a maddening waste of time. In the San Francisco Bay area, driving commutes can be 50 miles or more and 90 minutes one way, so we need to think about cars as the "third place" between home and work—places that enable productivity when one is stuck in traffic.

Disruptive innovations are taking the world of automotive transportation by storm: from ride sharing to self-driving cars, car data analytics and behavioral adjustments, to how vehicles are built, purchased, serviced, insured, navigated, and more. At a Churchill Club program in Silicon Valley titled "Disrupting Automotive Transportation," Johann "JJ" Jungwirth, president and CEO of Mercedes-Benz Research and Development North America, talked about how the company thinks about cars as mobility vehicles, that "third place," with intelligent and context-sensitive cars used for smart work wherever you are.[5]

Some of the greatest influences driving automotive change are within the digital space: the cloud, intelligence, analytics, contextual awareness, including the ecosystem around these devices and how we live our connected lives, as well as the physical ecosystem: what surrounds the outside of the car that influences our lives and automation. For example, Mercedes' "attention assist" feature sounds an alert to drivers and shows a little coffee cup on the dash when they are about to fall asleep at the wheel. The company's "intelligent drive" offers the most sophisticated and intelligent "stop-and-go pilot" and steering wheel assist, which works in low-speed traffic, where the car will autonomously follow the car ahead of it, brake and accelerate on its own, and maintain the appropriate desired distance—all leading to the next step: self-driving cars.

Additionally, the Mercedes will soon be able to pull contextual data based on the physical driving environment and the driver's personal routine and habits and then automate the vehicle to perform actions based on this data. For example, if you live in an area with harsh winters, your car would know to automatically turn on your seat and steering wheel warmers when it is below a certain temperature outside.

Mercedes also took some of its best technologies and put them into its least expensive cars. For example, in 2012, it introduced iPhone integration into the driving experience in the least expensive A-Class model, then in many other models. While you would anticipate the most advanced technologies to be integrated into the most expensive cars, Mercedes' leaders feel that it is very important for Millennials to have access to the technologies that are ingrained in their DNA.

In January 2015, Mercedes launched a global campaign to rethink the car as a third place: a place where you gain back time. Whether it is a personal, shared, or self-driving vehicle (where new business models will enable us to buy mileage packages instead of owning or leasing a vehicle), the automobile can become your "workplace, your video conferencing room, your living room, your concert hall, or lounge etc.—at any point in time whenever you want and/or need it," said Jungwirth.[6] Mercedes will be unveiling some unique interior designs that will make you ask: What took so long?

"In the end, it's about getting valuable time back. When you drive, commuting in the morning and night, it's just boring having to drive by yourself and pay attention to yourself. Think if you could get all that time back to interact with colleagues, friends, family via video conferencing or FaceTime, or have your car be a cinema . . . in that moment in time, that is huge," said Jungwirth.[7]

TO WORK FROM ANYWHERE . . .

"A company's perceived wealth and therefore power was for so long based on how much real estate it held," says Glenn Dirks, vice president of customer enablement at Better Workplace, a software provider that helps organizations improve performance through workforce mobility management. Every corporate employee used to need a dedicated place to work, so no one questioned the size of the corporate real estate portfolio. Today, with judicious use of technology, we can work from anywhere at any time. It is no longer about the height of a building, the big corner office, the ornate hallways, the mahogany desks. Yet in most large organizations today, 30 to 70 percent of vacant space is underutilized, according to Dirks. "The reality is that you walk around those spaces and realize there is little correlation with actual employee work behavior and the spaces they are provided."[8]

As an executive in charge of facilities at what was then Sun Microsystems, Dirks witnessed just how much money and time a company can save with processes like telecommuting. Sales executive Bill Passmore persuaded Scott McNealy, then CEO of Sun Microsystems, that global mobility and keeping workers close to where their customers are was more important than having a massive corporate office and regional headquarters around the world. And McNealy came to value mobility on a personal level after his own children were born, as he realized that life is enriched by spending more time, not less, with family. Before Sun was acquired by Oracle in 2010, 55 percent of its workforce worked from home, and the company ultimately saved $70 million annually in real estate. With the exception of management consulting firms, Sun was one of the first large real estate holders to adopt formal mobile work programs.

At Better Workplace, Dirks's new employer, the signature product is WorkFit, a survey questionnaire that assesses how employees are working in organizations and produces detailed reports to help organizations "align company resources to provide an optimal match with your employees' mobile work styles—lowering cost, improving performance, and increasing environmental efficiency," according to the company's website.[9]

In spite of all our technology and mobility, a stigma is still attached to people working from homes or coffee houses. Face time still trumps perceptions of how much time someone is putting in. According to Dirks, telework adoption is moving slowly because of middle-management resistance to change, cultural issues surrounding trust, and lack of the correct tools to fully mobilize employees.

PRODUCTIVITY BASED ON RESULTS, NOT FACE TIME

In a case study from the University of Minnesota, Kathleen D. Vohs, Joseph P. Redden, and Ryan Rahinel discovered that physical order produces healthy choices, generosity, and conventionality, whereas disorder produces creativity. In essence, the more creative and risk tolerant we want workers to be, the more we need to disrupt their work environment with flexible and varying work options.[10] How can we use these findings to shape our organizations into what we want them to be?

A study by the National Study of Employers in 2012 reported that 63 percent of companies surveyed are permitting at least some of their employees to work from home some of the time, as opposed to 34 percent just seven years earlier.[11] However, telework options are offered mostly to freelancers or contractors.

Left to their own devices, most people will do the right thing when they work outside the office, and companies have recourse when work is based on results, not face time. The billable hour and time clock is no longer about tracking employees through work chairs, keystrokes, or phone call logs, it is about ROWE (results-only work environment), and it all begins with the remote workplace.

Best Buy had a high-profile and instructive experience with ROWE. In 2005, CEO Brad Anderson wanted to try something radically different: allow corporate employees to control their schedules and how often they showed up at the company's Richfield, Minnesota, headquarters.[12] The company evaluated employees solely on performance rather than time worked and office attendance. The goal was to focus not on where people worked but on the quality of their work. If a guy can get his work done while fishing for marlin, is happier, and as a result is more productive, then who cares? If a woman can be at her kids' after-school activities yet still show more productivity (because the schedule is more conducive for her and her family), more power to her. What were the results? Best Buy leadership found that the turnover rate dropped from 17 to 3 percent per year. And, according to ROWE creators Cali Ressler and Jody Thompson, two former Best Buy employees whom Anderson encouraged to cofound CultureRx, a Minneapolis-based human resources consulting firm, ROWE saved the company over $2 million over a three-year period, mainly by greatly lowering voluntary employment turnover and by increasing productivity by an average of 41 percent.[13]

Yet Best Buy killed ROWE shortly after Herbert Joly became CEO in September 2012. Why? It is not entirely clear; the program saved the company millions, saw reduced rates in attrition, and created a happier work environment. In all fairness, not every person or particular skill set can work from home. Some people need and want to be micromanaged or to do the micromanaging, and some teams work far better when they are side by side, bouncing ideas and computer code off one another. Still, Ressler and Thompson diagnosed any problems at Best Buy corporate as due to a lack of leadership and poor management. Instead of issues with working remotely, they feel that ROWE "is being used as a scapegoat for other problems with the company."[14] In response, the ROWE inventors wrote a blog post that shredded Joly's decision to end ROWE, accusing Best Buy of returning to "last century management practices."[15]

As I stated earlier, some ideas in this book have already been tried and jettisoned, but I believe that, for a set of companies, this is the time to resurrect this thinking, and someone's failed leadership or poor management should never undermine what can be very advantageous to the bottom line. Other companies are showing interest in this flexible telework approach, buoyed by the belief that working from home—or at least having the option to—does significantly improve performance.

According to Families and Work Institute research, employees are overburdened with day-to-day expectations at work and at home and simply do not have enough time in the day to get everything done.[16] Lisa Horn, co-leader of the Society for Human Resource Management's Workplace Flexibility Initiative, explains that the increased stress levels are having an adverse effect on long-term health, creating more productivity issues for companies.[17] She believes that one of the major solutions to several productivity and cost-saving issues (real estate, recruiting, health absences) is to implement the right set of flexible work situations. According to Horn, it is this flexibility that attracts many top professionals who are looking to balance their life with their work, as 80 percent of professionals indicate that workplace flexibility is a determining factor to job decisions. Horn says that "employees with flexible arrangements are almost twice as likely to stay in current jobs and four times as likely to be highly engaged in their work."[18]

These claims were investigated in a *Harvard Business Review* study called "To Raise Productivity, Let More Employees Work from Home" conducted by Nicholas Bloom, professor of economics at Stanford University, and James Liang, cofounder of a leading travel service website in China called Ctrip. At Ctrip, the call center staff could volunteer to work from home for nine months. Half of the volunteers were allowed to telecommute, while the remainder of the control group remained at Ctrip's physical office space. Performance data, as well as survey data, was collected throughout the nine-month study.

The results of the study were astounding. What Ctrip leadership expected was cost savings on office space, furniture, and technology, but what they found was that employees who worked from home completed 13.5 percent more calls than did the staff that remained at the call center. Their increased productivity was the equivalent of almost a full extra workday a week. These at-home employees also quit at half the rate of the individuals in the office and reported a much higher level of job satisfaction. It was also estimated that Ctrip saved approximately $1,900 per employee on office furniture and space.[19] With these results, it's hard to imagine that ROWE or something like it won't be the future of work.

THE RISK FACTOR

The risk assessment in smart work is: What can we do to work smarter? And how will we use smarter work to elevate our ability to take risk? What are the least costly things we can do to reduce the attrition rate from 80 to 50 percent, for example? It is expensive to recruit, it is expensive to provide benefits, it is expensive to let someone go, and it is very expensive to hold an overabundance of real estate. What changes might mitigate any or all of these expenses?

The Unoffice

In Silicon Valley, common wisdom holds that work is something you do, not a place you go. Happily, the region is also full of flat organizations that were founded and are still deeply rooted in collaboration, trust, and engagement.

In 2011, the executives at Silicon Valley Bank were looking for ways to be more consistent with the culture they helped build, so they experimented with the "unoffice," where no one, including general partners, held a corner office or even any designated space. The concept is often referred to as "liquid space." Whenever anyone requires a place to meet, they can reserve a conference room through the mobile app. Given that the property, on Sand Hill Road, remains the most expensive commercial real estate in the country, averaging $111 per square foot (down from a peak of $144 to $198 per square foot in 2011), an unoffice approach seemed like an immediate, natural approach to cost savings.

The unoffice approach or something like it can work in a really large organization as well. Aetna, a leading managed healthcare company, uses flexible workspaces to boost its bottom line. Out of Aetna's 35,000 employees, 14,500 do not have a desk. This decision was made by CEO Mark Bertolini and national business chief Joseph Zubretsky to cut real estate costs. Another 2,000 employees work from home a few days week, making the teleworking workforce 47 percent of the total. Through telecommuting, the company has cut 2.7 million square feet of office, a savings of approximately $78 million annually, including utilities, housekeeping, mail service, and document shredding.[20]

Results Oriented—Imagine That!

One of the most talked about company documents over the last few years is a 126-page slide deck on company culture called "Netflix Culture: Freedom & Responsibility." The reason it's gotten so much attention is its results orientation and the way Netflix views its employees: not as a family but as a pro sports team where employees are hired, developed, and cut smartly, so the firm has the best players in every position. Slide 24, "The Keeper Test Managers Use," asks: "Which of my people, if they told me they were leaving in two months for a similar job at a peer company, would I fight hard to keep at Netflix?" Slide 25 states: "The other people should get a generous severance now, so we can open a slot to try to find a star for that role."[21]

Yet, as rewards for acting with a certain business acumen, Netflix leadership extends trust and freedom to employees. Netflix's model increases employee freedom so the company can continue to attract and nourish innovative people, thus enabling the firm to be nimble and adapt to exponential changes. Unlike most large organizations, Netflix believes that focusing on process drives more talent out, so it seeks solutions to simplify and streamline whatever processes are absolutely necessary. For example, employees are not measured by how many evenings or weekends they are in the office but by how much, how quickly, and how well they get their work done. Until 2004, Netflix offered the standard number of vacation days per year and tracked employees' time off. Yet internal research revealed that employees tend to work from their computers nights and weekends, responding to emails at odd hours, and that amount of extra time justified allowing people to take some personal time off. An employee pointed out to human resource personnel that since hours worked per day or per week aren't tracked, why are vacation days? Netflix leaders agreed to look into it and ultimately decided to focus on what gets done, not how many hours or days someone worked. Netflix does not have a 9-to-5 workday policy, nor does it have a vacation policy—its unlimited vacation policy recognizes that, more often than not, if employees are given the freedom, chances are they will opt to work or check in no matter where and when.

Netflix believes that its employees are responsible for ensuring that they live out Netflix's values. So, the company's values statement about expenses, entertainment, gifts, and travel policy, presented on slide 74, is five words long: "Act in Netflix's Best Interest." Akin to the honor code is the employee's pledge, listed on slide 28: "I will not lie, nor cheat, nor steal, nor tolerate those who do." This translates into employees expensing what is necessary for work, traveling as if using their own money, disclosing non-trivial vendor gifts, and "taking" from Netflix only when it is inconsequential to take or inefficient not to take. (According to slide 75, "'Taking' means, for example, printing personal documents at work or making personal calls on work phone: inconsequential and inefficient to avoid." According to slide 77, the goal is to "inhibit chaos with ever more high performance people," and "flexibility is more important than efficiency in the long term.")

Create Renewal Workspaces

Let people rest on the job. In the *New York Times* article titled "Relax! You'll Be More Productive," author Tony Schwartz reports that "researchers found that sleeping too little—defined as less than six hours each night—was one of the best predictors of on-the-job burn-out."[22] In a study in the *Journal of Occupational & Environmental Medicine* titled "The Cost of Poor Sleep: Workplace Productivity Loss and Associated Costs," the researchers estimate that $3,156 is lost in yearly productivity by those suffering from insomnia and an estimated $2,500 is lost by workers who are not getting enough sleep or have other sleep problems.[23]

The answer, according to Schwartz, is to set up renewal workspaces, such as yurts, napping rooms, or sprawling couches, where workers can regain energy and refocus their energies, all through quiet-time activities. These simple renewal practices contribute to a more productive workforce.

Time Off

Taking organizational or game-changing risk is exhausting, and it's often the very reason people need time to rest and recover after big projects. Recovery theory, a key pillar of athletic performance training, doesn't factor into the strategies of most companies. However, as we demand ever more consistent productivity and extraordinary moments of excellence from our employees, we need to better understand and utilize these proven practices.

There are three different categories of recovery:

1. **Immediate or short-term recovery.** The value of the cool-down phase in recovering from intense activities in performance-related activities, such as sports, has been proven. Muscles need time to repair and rejuvenate, with proper food and rest to aid the process. The same concept works within companies: Workers need recovery periods from

intense work where physical or mental energy was taxed heavily.

2. **Intermediate-term recovery.** Vacations and extended holidays are the primary methods organizations use to help workers' intermediate recovery, yet often these periods are considered more as employee benefits and not the productivity tools that performance science suggests they can be. Companies need to be attuned to the ebbs and flows of annual business cycles and incentivize workers to take time off during the periods immediately preceding higher-intensity periods.

3. **Long-term recovery.** After years of intense work, one- or two-week vacations are not sufficient to provide a complete physiological and psychological reset. Much as athletes take a month or more away from their sport when their competitive season is completed, a number of companies—including Adobe, Timberland, American Express, Nike, Blue Cross Blue Shield, Hallmark, and more than 100 others—have implemented paid employee sabbaticals.

According to data collected by YourSABBATICAL, a company that partners with businesses to design and integrate sabbaticals to retain talent, work sabbaticals benefit companies by helping retain valued employees, attract top talent, increase productivity, develop high potentials, revitalize workforces, and provide new experiences in risk-taking. YourSABBATICAL also notes that sabbaticals help workers build better self-awareness, replenish their energy, find renewed commitment to the job, have surges in creativity, and become inspiring presences to others.[24] Well-executed sabbaticals increase employees' perspective on the world and their sense of self and directly impact their ability to think outside the box. They create a better pool of knowledge among employees and help them gain an increased confidence in negotiating risk. A study done by Ernst & Young in 2006 with its workers showed that their performance ratings improved by 8 percent for every ten hours of additional vacation time taken.[25]

Play to Foster Creativity

We have known for years how important play is in the learning, maturation, and socialization of children. As I state in *Secrets of Silicon Valley,* "play is what develops design capabilities and the love of learning in our brains." So, why not allow adults the opportunity to continue to play games?

Perhaps your organization doesn't offer sprawling space for volley or bocce ball courts, but there are a myriad of ways to integrate gaming into the workplace. The important takeaway is that games are structured to provide feedback and invite better performance when repeated. According to Daniel Cook of Spry Fox, a video gaming production company, you can break the impacts of gaming down into four simple parts:

1. A player performs an action.
2. The action results in an effect.
3. The player received feedback.
4. This information allows players to perform more actions.[26]

These increased actions have the power to change human behavior. According to game designer Jesse Schell, frequent flyer points and cash-back programs are simply games that give something to aspire to and create loyalty behaviors.[27] For example, in the consumer world, Weight Watchers rewards points for playing the weight loss game. The Ford Fusion offers the ability to grow a virtual tree on your dashboard if you drive more economically, changing the way people drive.

This same concept is being used for employees, as a growing number of companies are using games to teach new skills; increase speed and efficiency; practice scenarios; gain work experience and knowledge in safe, controlled, and fun environments; and inspire new goals or creative thinking. By ramping up the maturation process through games and simulations, employees develop a better mastery of skills that allow them to improvise and engage in the types of calculated risk-taking that can increase agility and accelerate innovation.

CHAPTER EIGHT

Decision-Making amid the Clutter

Largely ignored by the investor community, Russia was overlooked in the first wave of the e-commerce boom. It stood on the sidelines and watched as money was being poured into the rest of the BRIC countries—Brazil, India, and China. Most investors and entrepreneurs felt that Russia was too corrupt, too unpredictable in its politics and business practices, and too underdeveloped to take the chance. Most American retailers—including Amazon, eBay, and Walmart—continue to stay away even today.

Meet Maelle Gavet. She is the CEO of Ozon, Russia's largest e-commerce site, frequently referred to as the Amazon of Russia. Building Ozon has been one enormous risk after another. The flip side is that it offered a hell of an opportunity to be the first to market in a near-untapped, massive market. The average income of Russia's population, over 143.5 million, has more than tripled since 2000. Regardless, being the first in Russia was a daunting task, as business decisions that would be utterly routine in most of the world are groundbreaking in Russia. For example, Russians are not accustomed to paying for products in advance of receiving them, and paying with a credit card online was unheard of. Even in 2014, only about 30 million credit cards are in circulation in the Russian population, according to Euromonitor International, in comparison, the average U.S. consumer has three open credit card accounts according to Experian, the credit card monitoring group. Accordingly, 80 percent of Ozon's sales are paid in cash on delivery; credit card payments make up a mere 10 percent. Getting products from point to point also proved to be a massive headache. Ozon had over 2,100 pickup points scattered over 130 cities and was capable of shipping to 75 percent of the Russian population, but there was no Russian-based FedEx or DHL equivalent, and the national mail service was unreliable. As a result, Gavet made a very bold move. She built out a private shipping company, O-Courier, to get products delivered consistently and on time.

This one decision was critical to Ozon's success. Ozon now operates 4,000 pickup points and the largest warehouse facility in Eastern Europe, second only to Amazon's German warehouse.[1] Gavet is now leveraging these innovative efforts to grow two new start-ups: Ozon.travel and Sapato.ru, which sells shoes (much like a Russian Zappos). "We want to build the biggest online player in Russia," Gavet said in a 2012 *Fast Company* article titled, "Is this the Jeff Bezos of Russia?"[2] Ozon is set to exceed $1 billion in revenue in 2014, according to Morgan Stanley, and is one of the most trusted brands in Europe. (In fact, 25 percent of Russian online shoppers state that Ozon is their favorite destination in part because of the trust factor.[3])

Gavet's big bet paid off, but if you were in her shoes, how would you have met these challenges? What decisions would you, your team, and your board of directors make? Would you be able to pull the trigger and be willing to put it all on the line?

Traditional definition of decision-making	Decisions often are made by the person who has the highest salary in the room, usually someone far removed from the customer or client.
Risk-taker's definition of decision-making	Every person—from the janitor to the administrative assistant to middle management to the CEO—is responsible for the success or failure of your organization. Collaborative decision-making and internal councils encourage engagement, foresight, and accuracy among the people who actually do the tasks.

DECISIONS, DECISIONS, DECISIONS . . .

Think about the hundreds of thousands of people who run in marathons each year. Less than 1 percent of those have the capability or even the desire to win the race. Elite-caliber racers "run to win," while the rest of the marathoners "live to run" and see training as a way to discover their best selves. Runners know that training for a marathon—nutrition, sleep, tapering (reducing your mileage leading up to the marathon), gear, race strategy, and the like—is critical to the outcome on race day. But equally important is the execution of that strategy—the thousands of improvised decisions made throughout the race, such as "Should I speed up to pass that guy?" "Should I eat my energy gel now or wait a couple more miles?" "How should I navigate that upcoming hill or bend in the road?" "It might rain, so should I keep on my windbreaker or discard it?" Weather, wardrobe, course conditions, sleep, other racers, your own physical condition the day of the race—there are a myriad of variables that are in your control and others that are not. These decisions, seemingly trivial in the moment, have huge effects in the last third of a marathon. This is the time when your body and mind are fatigued as you "hit the wall" (that point in the marathon where a runner feels like he or she can no longer sustain his or her race pace), and an earlier decision to speed up by ten seconds per mile has caused you to cramp up with miles still to go. These decisions can mean the difference between finishing with your hands over your head with a new personal record and ending hours later in the "marathon shuffle," exhausted and defeated.

LET'S GET REAL

There is no doubt that organizations struggle with decision-making, and increasingly so. In command and control environments, decisions tend to be left to an executive team whose members think they know what is best across the organization. In chaotic, free-flowing environments, decisions can be tough to come by, because unless there is a formal process in place, people make decisions in a vacuum and often don't share them with their most valuable team members. Some senior to middle managers have shared with me that decisions are mostly made by the highest-paid person in the room, often people who are far removed from the customer or the client. We do have to learn and relearn that every person contributes to the success or failure of the organization, and for the most part, the people who are closest to the job, client, or customer are the ones most qualified to make a decision. Of course, decision-making requires a process and appropriate timing.

THE IMPORTANCE OF TIMING

We assume that an excellent decision is timeless. This leads to a lack of understanding of what indecision, or the absence of action, can cause. Procrastination, distraction, and general malaise all keep average professionals from making sound decisions, which can mean lost opportunity and even disaster.

The timing of risk and follow-up actions are often critical to the success of the decision. The emergence of a new technology, the misfortune of a competitor, the passing of new laws or abolition of old ones, and hundreds of other events over which you have no control can affect the environment. Intuition and feel can be just as important as data analysis in spotting these forces. Great risk-takers act at the most opportune time by collecting information and pooling knowledge from other trusted advisors, in combination with their own experiences and driving interests.

Across the board, there is a growing sense of frustration about how long companies take to make—or not make—decisions. In a 2009 *McKinsey Quarterly* survey, "Flaws in Strategic Decision Making," only 28 percent of over 2,200 executives surveyed ranked the quality of strategic decision-making as good. The results were astonishing in that 60 percent of the executives felt that bad decisions were fairly rampant and were made as frequently as good decisions.[4] Now, one person's bad decision can be another person's excellent decision, but research reveals that it's becoming increasingly difficult to hit in the "good decision" range.

In a November 2013 *Harvard Business Review* article titled "You Can't Be a Wimp—Make the Tough Calls," *HBR* senior editor Melinda Merino asked Ram Charan, a preeminent advisor to CEOs and boards, "What has changed the most over the years about how executives make decisions?" Charan, who wrote the book *Conquering a Culture of Indecision,* brings up what we all think about but have difficulty encapsulating—the magnitude of what's on our plates. According to Charan, making decisions in today's world is tougher because we are operating with a greater number of variables in exponential times, many of these variables being highly ambiguous, and often judged on a world stage, which didn't exist a decade ago.[5] He states:

> You're wrestling with more qualitative factors, with no conventional methodology, under the real threat that part of your business has peaked or could become irrelevant. Meanwhile, enormous opportunities that require big bets arise and vanish quickly. And any decision you make will be judged in the court of public opinion. You have to take into account potential consequences for a range of constituencies who may have no direct long-term economic interest in the business—regulators, shareholder activities, societal watchdogs, the media. These conditions were beginning to emerge 10 years ago, but now they're dominant.[6]

Charan doesn't address another factor that has enormous influence in any decision-making process: corporate culture. As you have seen in the Why Risk-Taking Isn't Gambling chapter, workplaces run the risk continuum, from command and control all the way to autonomous chaos. Regardless of where an organizational culture stands on the spectrum, it is nearly impossible to mitigate risk in strategic decision-making. In controlled cultures, most people will do the same thing over and over, sticking to core comforts, and no new decisions get made. In a culture of autonomy, you can maximize possibility, but the left hand often doesn't know what the right is doing, and making decisions can be exhausting and debilitating.

Consider the range of occupations and the degree of risks involved. A nuclear power plant operator, for example, will make static, straight-line decisions, which is exactly what you want him or her to do—we don't want any risk if a particular procedure is already deemed safe. Organizational leaders, however, are being paid, we hope, to make risky decisions. Most environments and tasks demand something between static and utter chaos. Someone who is daring by nature may need some boundaries, and someone who is overly cautious may need to integrate some chaos. Remember that chaos can spawn true genius but also trigger catastrophe. In fact, the difference between genius and catastrophe is often defined solely by the timing of the risk. So, how do we identify the specific moment in which a decision to take risk is worth taking?

WHEN DECISIONS CANNIBALIZE YOUR EXISTING LINES OF REVENUE

Sometimes big decisions are painful, particularly if you are risking cannibalizing an existing product's revenue stream by introducing another product intended for complementary use. In 2001, NetApp had to make one such bold decision. Customers were frustrated with how long it took to back up data to tape (typically all weekend on large systems, and often longer, which would impact production work), and how arduous (and often unreliable) restores from tape were. Needless to say, customers weren't happy about the loss of productivity, especially as business application demands became 24/7.

Several NetApp employees understood the data backup-restore problem, and they firmly believed NetApp could develop a good solution by leveraging the existing product line. Two NetApp product managers, in collaboration with an outside consultant and with the support of key managers, developed a compelling business case for a "nearline data disk drive–based storage system" targeted for data backup and restore and data archiving use.[7] The system used ATA (advanced technology attachment) disk drives instead of the fibre channel (FC) disk drives that were the standard for enterprise-class storage systems.

ATA disk drives were the mainstay storage in personal computers; they were not considered to be reliable enough for, nor able to provide the performance needed by, enterprise storage arrays. ATA disk drives were chosen for the nearline system because they provided denser storage capacity and a lower cost per GB than FC drives. Those characteristics were crucial to delivering a disk drive–based system that could displace tape library use for data backup and restore. The business plan for the nearline system was approved and the product was called NearStore.

NearStore provided the opportunity to capture significant new revenue. While some customers were using NetApp's mainstream FC systems, they were too expensive and capacity-limited for most customers to adopt in place of tape-based backup and restore. However, launching NearStore also presented a risk that some customers would purchase it instead of one or more of NetApp's FC systems in an effort to reduce storage expense.[8] This risk was embraced with the sober understanding that sooner or later ATA-based storage systems (like NearStore) would be used for more mainstream enterprise data storage use. Strategically, it was much better for NetApp to lead this evolution and cannibalize its own product revenue rather than have a competitor do it.

Introducing NearStore also presented other challenges. Although it was targeted for backup-restore and data archival use, NearStore's specs and features would be compared to more capable mainstream enterprise storage systems, by both prospective customers and competitors. It was critical to NearStore's success that its functionality and benefits instead be compared to tape libraries, which were the established enterprise backup-restore and archive solution, instead of mainstream enterprise storage arrays.

NetApp first introduced NearStore with a price point in between that of high performance disk drives and lower-cost tape units. While tape was, and remains, a cost-competitive backup media, NearStore provided faster and more reliable backups and data restores. It was able to demonstrate that the use of NetApp's SnapVault and SnapMirror technology reduced the physical storage requirements for backup data by up to 95 percent. Unsure how customers would respond, the company held its breath.

Secondary storage turned out to be a gold mine for NetApp, using the NearStore as the target for backups and other secondary copies. "As you can see, there was no separate 'earlier product' that was being cannibalized; it was NetApp's entire primary product line. In my view, NearStore actually opened up a new market for us . . . a market we created," said a NetApp marketing executive.[9] NearStore became a big business opportunity, rather than a near-term (or even long-term) risk. There's no question that the revenue and margin dollars produced by NearStore over the first 3+ years were additive to NetApp's finances. After four quarters, by January 2003, NearStore made up a significant percentage of NetApp's revenue and continued to grow. As important as NearStore was to the growth of NetApp's sales and market share, its strategic value was even greater. NearStore provided avenues for NetApp to win business from and establish relationships with new customers who were then buying from their competition; it helped get NetApp in the back door and broaden their presence for newer avenues for storage. NearStore was focused on providing a better solution, and while it was a nail-biting time for the decision-makers, they all look back and know that sometimes tough decisions can enable a big win.

How Little and Big Data Is Changing Decision-Making

For more than one hundred years, baseball had been led by "baseball men." These scouts were largely grizzled veterans who evaluated players based on intangibles like momentum and "feel" or even how much they looked like prototypical baseball players, using statistics such as stolen bases, runs batted in, and batting average, relics of a nineteenth-century view of the game and the information available at that time. Then came Billy Beane.

The Oakland A's operated with one of the lowest payrolls in baseball. Through economic necessity, Beane judged players not on how they looked but by how they statistically performed in overlooked areas that increased chances of scoring runs. He loved players who got on base by being walked, which was not something the baseball men favored, and he discouraged base stealing, which statistically decreased run-scoring activity. By crunching data in novel ways to make decisions that others did not understand, Beane creating a winning team that outperformed most others with payrolls up to four times larger. The information Beane used, you might say, was "little data." Now we are in the world of big data.

At first, the furor over big data might be confusing. After all, humans have been gathering data since the dawn of civilization: You gather information, test, and deduce that something is worth noting—such as fire is hot and will burn you—and you share this with others. The reason that big data is so impactful is its enormous potential for expediting decision-making when a massive amount of data is involved. Big data typically is defined as "the ability to sort and query through expanding oceans of digital information"—in other words, to detect, analyze, and make assumptions (not conclusions) on highly diffused patterns.[10]

Information technology and data analysis have long been used to automate routine, day-to-day operational decisions, such as logistics and inventory management, personalized marketing offers and recommendations, and fraud detection. For example, when traveling in another country, a bank card user often receives an automated email or phone call asking for verification of a transaction.

The amount of data available today is so massive, due to the increase in people online and the invention of social media and user-generated content, that according to Zettaset, a big data security company, the world daily creates 2.5 quintillion bytes of data, and about 90 percent of what's out there has been created just in the last couple of years.[11] Such a large and complex quantity of digitally stored information simply can't be managed with day-to-day computer processing tools.

David Hausler, an expert in bioinformatics and genomics at University of California, Santa Cruz, offers an example of what big data can accomplish in practice. In the quest for an effective cancer drug, you have to be able to share vast amounts of patterns of mutations that are common to certain cancers that occur over and over. With big data, Hausler states, "Now we know that there's a certain type of patient who has this pattern of mutation, then we can figure out what genes are disrupted, and how we would approach treating that patient's special type of cancer. We call this precision medicine. Instead of giving everyone chemotherapy, we want a precise treatment that is targeting the particular patterns of mutations in a patient's tumor."[12]

According to Joe Hersch's article on big data in a Santa Cruz publication called *Good Times Weekly,* in which Hausler was interviewed, each genome file—the DNA record from a tumor or a normal tissue—is 300 billion bytes. Hausler says, "Multiply 300 billion by the number of tissue samples. . . . And note that there are 1.2 million new cases of cancer every year in the United States—that's a lot of data. So, we work very hard to work out the technology for how we would actually store and manage all of this vital data . . . those two are intricately intertwined."[13]

Big data and data science can also help with strategic decision-making by allowing executives to see things from new viewpoints and assimilate complex concepts. Dave Snowden and Mary Boone's article "A Leader's Framework for Decision Making," in the *Harvard Business Review,* suggests that a framework can be defined with examples from the organization's history. "This enhances communication and helps executives rapidly understand the context in which they are operating." A very good framework, they write, is designed to help leaders determine the overall context for making their strategic decisions, in particular whether it is *ordered* and *complicated* or *unordered* and *complex.* "Each domain requires different actions," write Snowden and Boone. "*Simple* and *complicated* contexts assume an ordered universe, where cause-and-effect relationships are perceptible, and right answers can be determined based on the fact. *Complex* and *chaotic* contexts are unordered—there is no immediate relationship between cause and effect, and the way forward is determined based on emerging patterns. The ordered world is the world of fact-based management; the unordered world represents pattern-based management."[14]

LinkedIn's success is due, in part, to its finding patterns. Jonathan Goldman, a PhD in physics from Stanford, examined why the site's almost 8 million users (at the time) were not connecting with each other at levels the LinkedIn team had originally expected. He started studying people's connections and seeking out patterns that eventually allowed him to predict the future connections in established LinkedIn networks. Reid Hoffman, LinkedIn's cofounder, was a huge fan of analytics through his success at PayPal, and he unleashed Goldman to make changes. So Goldman started experimenting with a new function that would suggest names of people someone hadn't yet connected with, but would seem likely to know, such as classmates from schools, members of shared professional groups, and coworkers at the same companies. He created the "triangle closing"—the notion that if you know Jennifer and Bill, Jennifer and Bill have a higher likelihood of knowing each other. LinkedIn's "People You May Know" feature has helped it generate millions of new connections, driving a remarkable increase in activity on its website.

IBM'S WATSON

Named after IBM founder Thomas J. Watson, Watson was developed in IBM's research labs in 2005. IBM's Watson is known as a *cognitive system,* meaning it is able to learn and interact more naturally with people. Rather than relying on programming, as traditional computers do, cognitive systems are able to think, learn, and navigate the complexity of human language. This enables cognitive systems to understand their users' needs and the context of their questions. Of course, unlike humans, cognitive systems can also read through millions of pages of unstructured data in seconds to uncover evidence-based insights that assist users. Watson is also able improve its performance with every interaction and outcome, as it builds its data-driven knowledge and learns all about users' realms of expertise.

David Ferrucci, who served as the principal lead of Watson, and many other contributors were involved in the system's development, including IBM researchers to experts from eight universities, set a heady milestone for Watson. How would the cognitive system fair answering questions on the game show *Jeopardy* (competing against human champions Ken Jennings and Brad Rutter)? While the entire Internet and various other encyclopedia-type sources were downloaded onto Watson, the game show environment truly tested Watson's ability to handle the nuances of human language, to quickly analyze a lot of information about a lot of things, to put it in the appropriate context, and then to play the game by buzzing in on time and wagering to its benefit.

The contest, which was taped on January 13, 2011, at IBM's T. J. Watson Research Laboratory in front of an audience of IBM executives and company clients, played out over three televised episodes. For the IBM team, it was a nail-biter. Watson was in a tie with Rutter, at $5,000 each, with Jennings trailing with $2,000, but by the end of the show, Watson pulled off a win and took home the $1 million prize. IBM donated the money to two charities, World Vision, a humanitarian organization focused on the needs of impoverished children and their families, and World Community Grid, a public computing grid focused on solving some of humanity's greatest challenges such as a cure for HIV and cancer and affordable water purification.[15]

Now Watson is cloud based, with connections from handheld apps and online services that allow for ease of access. Watson's focus isn't on *simplifying* workplace decision-making; rather, it's about *strengthening* decision-making with insights gleaned from crunching massive amounts of data. This capability will become more important for every business operating today. About 80 percent of the information created and used by enterprises, including documents, public tweets, articles and journals, and healthcare records, is unstructured. Within this data lies information that can help businesses identify new markets and revenue opportunities and medical organizations improve care and save lives. This is where Watson's capabilities shine.

In a news release, IBM announced the establishment of the Watson Group:

> a new business unit dedicated to the development and commercialization of cloud-delivered cognitive innovations. . . . IBM will invest more than $1 billion into the Watson Group . . . this will include $100 million available for venture investments to support IBM's recently launched ecosystem of start-ups and businesses that are building a new class of cognitive apps powered by Watson.[16]

THE RISK FACTOR

In most organizations, many kinds of decisions need to be made regularly. These include operational decisions that are highly structured and oriented to the short-term and strategic decisions that set long-term directions and policies and are generally made by top management. In between are decisions about process—how to create greater efficiencies—as well as nonroutine decisions in response to daily issues. I discuss different tactics that can be applied to decision-making. The ones you find yourself using the most are probably the foundation for your decision-making process. Decision-making is almost never intuitive. It is imperative for organizations to design a protocol for decision-making.

Collaborative Decision-Making

Executive team decision-making is nothing new, but Amazon has a unique approach. Nadia Shouraboura, former head of supply chain and fulfillment at Amazon, was part of the S Team, a small group of people who make all the decisions at the company. In working with Jeff Bezos and about eight other people at the executive VP or VP levels, Shouraboura reviewed six-page documents on strategic opportunities or senior-level hires. Team members openly discussed their feelings about each decision without any retribution, as Bezos mandated a "consent and dissent" decision-making culture, meaning the team either executed or jettisoned every document it reviewed.[17]

In organizations, collaborative decision-making is key, but it can expand way beyond executive management. Done correctly, it ensures that ideas constantly flow, build on each other, and result in an end goal or product that's exponentially better than the original idea. A good idea is a good idea, but a good idea honed and refined by multiple minds might just become a great—and an executable—one.

Crowdsourced Decision-Making

Crowdsourced decision-making assumes that collective thinking can enhance an idea or solution. In fact, it believes that many ideas and solutions have yet to be imagined.

Crowdsourced decision processes foster the ability to:

- Look at the problem from different perspectives.
- Imagine what you could do if there were no barriers.
- Seek large quantities of ideas from diverse sources.
- Create models, demos, prototypes, or illustrations of ideas.

They also address the questions:

1. How open is the person to new experiences and to taking risks?
2. How much knowledge and passion does the person have to create new ideas?
3. How much time and resources does the person have to make his or her ideas happen?

James Surowiecki's book *The Wisdom of Crowds* tells the story of Sir Francis Galton, who attended a contest to guess the correct weight of an ox at a livestock fair in 1906. The nearly 800 competitors included more knowledgeable types, including butchers and farmers. As an average, the crowd had guessed that the ox weighed 1,197 pounds. Amazingly, the correct answer was 1,198 pounds.[18] Not one single guess came as close as the group's average guess. Lior Zoref, a self-described, crowd wisdom researcher, wished to replicate this experiment at a TED (Technology, Entertainment, Design) conference by bringing an ox onstage and asking the audience to guess its weight. What were the results? Out of 500 guesses, the lowest was 308 pounds, the highest more than 8,000 pounds, and the average was 1,792. The ox actually weighed 1,795 pounds.[19]

According to Surowiecki:

> Under the right circumstances, groups are remarkably intelligent, and are often smarter than the smartest people in them.
>
> Groups do not need to be dominated by exceptionally intelligent people in order to be smart. Even if most of the people within a group are not especially well-informed or rational, it can still reach a collectively wise decision. This is a good thing, since human beings are not perfectly designed decision makers. Instead, we are what the economist Herbert Simon called "boundedly rational." We generally have less information than we'd like. We have limited foresight into the future. Most of us lack the ability—and the desire—to make sophisticated cost-benefit calculations. Instead of insisting on finding the best possible decision, we will often accept one that seems good enough. And we often let emotion affect our judgment. Yet despite all these limitations, when our imperfect judgments are aggregated in the right way, our collective intelligence is often excellent.[20]

Surowiecki also found crowdsourcing is particularly effective in the following ways:

1. Demonstrating that there is more than one right answer.

2. Bringing people together is just as important as obtaining a goal because unexpected results may occur.
3. When people lack confidence, they can greatly benefit by working together.

Surowiecki also recognizes the weaknesses of groups in situations that do not encourage wide ranges of opinions and perspectives. The Bay of Pigs decision—the failed U.S. military invasion of Cuba that intended to overthrow the revolutionary left-wing government of dictator Fidel Castro on April 17, 1961—for instance, was driven by a dynamic psychologists call "group think," which yields results no better, on average, than individual decision-making. Even groups of experts work properly only when they allow space for dissenting voices.

The Gamification of Decision-Making

Gamification is defined by taking elements that make up a game—fun, play, challenge, design, transparency—and applying them to real-world objectives. In a business setting, it can be integrated into solutions for everything, including office tasks, training, marketing, and direct customer interaction. Gamification can be applied to solve a myriad of complex problems in government as well.

Luke Hohmann, founder and CEO of Conteneo, a collaboration amplification company grounded in the science of play, was tasked with finding a solution for the city of San Jose, California. In 2011, San Jose was facing a nearly intractible problem: It was staring down another year of a projected $100 million budget deficit "in the middle of ten straight years of budget deficits."[21] How should the mayor, Chuck Reed, and the members of the city council respond? They were plagued with decisions that needed to be settled in order to reconcile the budget shortfalls. Should they: Close libraries and community services? Continue to allow critical infrastructure to degrade by deferring repairs? Cut even more deeply into police and fire departments? The magnitude of the problem was overwhelming. As Mayor Reed suggested, the only path forward was to engage citizens in the process.

San Jose pioneered this technique, known as participatory budgeting, through its annual neighborhood association budget priority session. Previously, this session was structured as an informational meeting, in which the mayor and the city manager would make presentations and solicit resident feedback through a silent voting process. While this process provided real-time results, it failed to engage residents in substantive dialogue on challenges facing the city that were critical to finding a path forward in the budget crises.

By 2011, the challenges were so severe that the city decided to try something radically different: a serious game designed by Conteneo. Dubbed the budget game, it was based on a version of the game "Buy a Project" used by many of Silicon Valley's high-tech firms when trying to decide how to prioritize strategic projects.

In this game, residents were assembled in groups of seven people. Each group was given two sheets: A green sheet contained funding proposals, such as funding a library or funding gang prevention services. A red sheet contained revenue-generating proposals or cost cuts. To acquire the money to purchase an item on a green sheet, residents had to unanimously agree on an item on the red sheet. Once this agreement was reached, facilitators would distribute the money equally to the residents, who were then free to spend it on whichever proposal they wished.

For example, in the 2013 game, one of the red sheet items was increasing business taxes by $10 million while another was reducing the children's health initiative by $1 million. If the seven residents at a table unanimously agreed to these proposals, each resident would then be given $1,571,000 to spend (roughly the $11 million saved divided by 7). Collectively, the residents could then choose how to spend this money on such funding options as "Add 21 Community Service Officers" for $2.1 million or "Increase Hub Community Center Hours" for $900,000. Conteneo's Certified Collaboration Architects, a global team of trained facilitators, guide residents through the negotiations to draw out motivations driving the decisions.

Over the past four years, San Jose has implemented more than 80 percent of the recommendations made by residents playing these games, which demonstrates the extraordinary power that collaborative, serious games have in strategic budgeting, prioritization, and decision-making as a whole.

CHAPTER NINE

Branding and Marketing Noise

In gambling, you have to bet big to win big.

Hard as it is to believe now, there was once a time, early in his career, when Sir Richard Branson could not get the media to pay attention to him or his stores, Virgin Records. Accordingly, Branson planned something bold and daring—to make the first transatlantic crossing in a hot air balloon as tall as a 22-story building. On July 4, 1987, taking off from Maine, the "Virgin Atlantic Flyer" traveled 2,900 miles in a record-breaking time of 33 hours and reached speeds in excess of 130 mph before it crashed one mile off the coast of Scotland.[1] Both Branson and his copilot, Per Lindstrand, were rescued at sea by the Royal Navy, and Branson soon became known as the undisputed king of the publicity stunt.

Decades later, digital and social media creates a very noisy world for marketers and the rest of us. At the writing of this book, there is enough Internet traffic—every hour—to fill 7 million DVDs, and if you joined those DVDs side by side, they'd scale Mount Everest 95 times.

In order to match Branson's undisputed kingship of publicity, someone had not only to push the envelope out of the universe but also to be strategic enough to marry efforts inside and outside of digital and social media. Along came an Austrian-based energy drink company called Red Bull that wanted to spin brand marketing on its head and invite consumers to join it on an aspirational journey. In 1989, it started partnering with extreme athletes, asking them, "How can Red Bull partner with you to make you a better athlete?" Athletes such as snowboarder Shaun White, motorsports competitor Travis Pastrana, and surfer Carissa Moore jumped on board and worked with Red Bull to take their athleticism to the next level. In the process, Red Bull not only brought its product directly to its target customer but helped bring these sports, which were once considered on the fringe of extreme sports, more into mainstream.

Then, in 2012, Red Bull created the most unimaginable stunt of all time. On October 14, Red Bull Stratos transcended human limits when Austrian skydiver Felix Baumgartner climbed 128,100 feet into the stratosphere over New Mexico in a helium balloon before free-falling 24 miles in a pressure suit and parachuting to Earth at an estimated 833.9 mph (the photo at the beginning of the chapter).[2] Not only was the Stratos the moon shot for this generation of adventure seekers, but it also had incredible return on investment for the science community by pushing the human body to the outer limits.

Red Bull took an estimated $30 million risk with Stratos (about one-tenth of its annual marketing spend). The company understood the synergy between an out-of-Earth event and its branding and marketing continuity. Red Bull Stratos embodies what the energy drink is: bold, high-charging, and daring aspiration.

According to an article in *The Australian* titled "Felix Baumgartner's Plunge from Stratosphere Breaks Broadcast Records," Red Bull organizers claim that the live event was broadcast by more than "40 television networks in 50 countries and was streamed by more than 130 digital outlets." The first picture of Baumgartner appeared on Facebook showing him on his knees in the desert and was shared nearly 30,000 times in 30 minutes. The social media frenzy continued as Twitter reported that the event generated more than 3.1 million tweets.[3] The jump hit the brand message in its sweet spot. Red Bull took ownership of a very powerful space in advertising, which is to capture the imagination of the very customers it is built to delight. By creating an event that was singular and unique, Red Bull tapped the potential of new market segments for the energy drink company. "'The sponsorship transcended sports and entertainment into pop culture, hitting new consumers that Red Bull does not usually capture, and on a global scale,' said Ben Sturner, president and CEO of Leverage Agency, a sports, entertainment and media marketing company. . . . Red Bull Stratos will continue to be talked about and passed along socially for a very long time."[4] That is not bad for a so-called publicity stunt.

Traditional definition of branding/marketing	Communicating the value of the product in a way that the customer can relate to, for the purpose of selling that product or service.
Risk-taker's definition of branding/marketing	Convey three elements: (1) a logo that distinctly speaks your culture; (2) a market where your customer is; and (3) a plan to build community and social currency.

In the traditional sense, marketing is about figuring out what people want and building a product around it. In one respect, this is easier than it has ever been. And getting the word out has never been cheaper or more efficient. Conversely, white noise now fills every part of people's lives, and because of that, we feel unsure of what and who to believe and therefore more likely to tune out. In this content, data-saturated world, marketing messages lie mostly in the sea of the utterly forgettable, punctuated by brief moments of the instantly viral. It's a catch-22: Try to leverage your brand in predictable, un-exciting ways, and you lose; attempt something too bold and make a mistake, and your brand takes a viral hit it may not recover from.

The result is that consumer brand marketing must now be a truly organic beast, not a stream of pithy marketing messages. Information and communication has been democratized, so brand equity has become a volatile issue for most companies. It used to be based on a target market, but now people are connected by cohorts that transcend generations through their hobbies, passions, and interests. Because of this shift, brand equity is simultaneously one of the ultimate springs for future opportunity and a potential minefield that can end a company's life.

In the consumer space, the branding and marketing issues that offer significant upsides for companies willing to take a little risk include: declaration, pricing, timing and delivery, customer service, quality, markets, leverage, and influence.

Declaration

A brand needs to stand for something that resonates. Most people are defined to a large degree by the brands they are loyal to: the team they cheer for, the band they listen to, the car they drive, and so on. The brand defines values and lifestyles of those in a community. Connecting with the right community is not about finding the brand's members and then overloading them with ads. Think of building a brand more as a construction project, building trust over time by consistently adding value through conversations and deeds, helping inspire your community and doing so with your beliefs and values embroidered on both sleeves. So declare what you stand for.

Make the declaration clear and simple but fresh enough that people want to actively identify with it. Red Bull is the perfect example of a company declaring what they stand for.

Pricing

Some brands are directly tied to their pricing and payment structures. For example, JCPenney discovered how true this was when it abandoned running regular sales for a more consistent pricing policy. Its loyal client base quickly left in droves. Walmart asked Vlasic to make a gallon jar of pickles, then sold the jars at such a discount that the entire Vlasic brand was adversely affected for years. On the flip side, Starbucks used pricing as a way of transforming coffee from an everyman's cheap drink to a status drink worthy of the wallets of connoisseurs.

Timing and Delivery

How and when you deliver products must be managed like a perfectly orchestrated comedian's joke: Timing is everything. When Nest Labs first introduced its revolutionary thermostat, consumers signed up on a months-long waiting list. The wait helped drive the "in-demand" image, elevating its level of cool. The delivery method often is equally important. Netflix killed Blockbuster by betting on Internet/home delivery first, then by investing heavily in streaming services. FedEx and UPS have eaten the U.S. Postal Service's lunch, concentrating on package delivery, while the USPS continued to focus on ground-based letter delivery, which is being killed off by electronic billing and online catalogs. Amazon is exploring using drones to get as close as possible to near real-time delivery.

Customer Service

All too often, companies send a clear signal to customers about how much they really care about them through their customer service efforts (or lack thereof). I have a friend who bought thousands of dollars of furniture from a well-known, national store. The spring broke on one of his chairs, and he called to inquire about repair. Several calls went unreturned. When he finally raised a fuss, it was explained that his order record had been lost in the company's computer system upgrade and that he would need to wait until it was resolved. This friend, who had been a loyal word-of-mouth marketing source for the company, shared his extreme unhappiness with everyone he talked to in person and via social media. Another example is the now-famous United Airlines guitar debacle, where a flyer witnessed his very expensive Taylor guitar being thrown around by a baggage handler. The song he wrote, "United Breaks Guitars," which trashed the airline for damaging his guitar, became a huge viral hit on YouTube. Great customer service has become rare enough that when customers receive great service, they tend to treat it as an anomaly. With their no-hassle return policies, both Nordstrom and Zappos have become known for having the best customer service.

Quality

Quality still counts. If any one factor plays a key role in the sustainability of brand loyalty, it is the perceived quality of the product. The jeweler Tiffany & Co. has built a loyal empire due to the quality of its brands (unwilling to go cheaper and faster in its production or packaging), white-glove customer service, beautiful storefronts, and memorable packaging. Legendary motorcycle company Harley-Davidson recovered from its near-fatal purchase by AMF in 1969. After the acquisition, AMF made bad decisions to cut corners on quality and lend the Harley-Davidson name to other unrelated products, including golf carts. In 1981, Harley was rescued by a group of savvy investors, who focused on raising the quality of its motorcycles and rebuilding its brand mystique. They helped build regular HOG (Harley Owners Groups) rallies and tapped bike owners' ideas for customization for future bike models.

Markets

In today's world of personalization, niches are often stronger than general markets. Many of the strongest brands started with niche markets, with buyers who remain true to those niches with an almost cultlike fanaticism. A great example is Under Armour, a company founded by former University of Maryland football player Kevin Plank. He started by developing a wicking fabric for football undergarments, then continued to concentrate on high-quality football gear. Under Armour has leveraged its brand position to move into other sports markets while keeping its excellent brand recognition in the lucrative football market.

Leverage

Understand where your brand stands so you know how much you can leverage that brand recognition for a new product or service. It is important to know who values your brand the most versus having a general indifference to the brand name. As Harley-Davidson's venture into the golf cart world shows, often it is too much to expect consumers who already recognize the brand's inherent qualities to make the leap with you to another category. Pierre Cardin, once a highly prized upscale couture brand, squandered much of its hard-earned reputation by unsuccessfully chasing the mass market. Richard Branson understands that his brand is not about music, or air travel, or mobile phones . . . Virgin stands for quality cool, fostered by the charismatic founder's maverick and swashbuckling style.

Influence

Is your brand powerful enough to influence others? In his book *Social Physics,* Alex "Sandy" Pentland describes how science has shown that we are most heavily influenced by our social connections. People live within several different networks of social connections—family, places of worship, clubs, neighbors, and others. Brands that permeate these cross-networks become an important part of the social fabric. By incentivizing people to influence others in their social sphere, your brand can gain greater social status.

THE CMO'S ROLE IS CHANGING

Over the last decade, CMOs have paid a heavy price to learn that maintaining customer loyalty can be a little like herding cats. Many brands made a mad dash to overconcentrate on marketing through social media sites, such as Twitter and Facebook. The marketing world quickly learned how fleeting the impact of social media is in an overabundant marketplace. Validating the impact of marketing dollars remains a challenge for marketing frontrunners. "The CMO Survey," a biannual survey of CMOs supported by the American Marketing Association, McKinsey & Co., and Duke University, reveals that 49.2 percent of CMOs said that they could not measure any clear impact from their social media campaigns; nor could they measure the return on investment for such efforts. Tellingly, only 15.9 percent felt that they could prove that their social media campaigns were effectively adding benefits to their marketing efforts. However, marketers are predicting that companies will increase their overall social media marketing spend from 9.4 to 21.4 percent over the next five years.[5]

To meet the increasing social and digital nature of customers' expectations for brands on both a rational and emotional level, CMOs have turned to the science of data. And what they are discovering has provided fertile ground for taking new approaches in marketing.

The role of marketing is evolving into a more strategic weapon, with analytics providing the ammunition. Analytics is the language of finance, IT, and business unit leaders, and marketers need to master it if they want to be influential within the company, says Matt Jauchius, CMO of Nationwide Insurance.[6] Due to the rise of computing power and the affordability of stored data, big data and analytics are providing the biggest promise for new streams of marketing opportunities. Instead of asking customers what they believe they would do, we can now track actual behavior by tracking billions of digital actions each day. We can see not only the real customer behaviors in action but how social connections can influence behaviors. This type of data promises to provide highly focused marketing that anticipates needs and delivers more effective communication to customers.

Customer relationship management (CRM) tools came into their own in the 1990s, with almost every company investing in them. Now with the rapid emergence of big data analytics tools, we are experiencing a second wave of CRM potential. In an article in *The Economist* titled "Less Guff, More Puff," Marco Rimini of Mindshare, a global media and marketing services company, was quoted as saying, "Now you see CRM methodology in places where it had not been applied before." *The Economist* added that marketers "can now establish direct relationships. The more marketers learn, the more they will tailor their [operations and communications] to what they think shoppers want."[7]

Gilt Groupe cofounder Alexis Maybank shares how data is essential for the online e-commerce site. "Now we have almost five years of data on most of our members and customers, so we're able to do more nuanced marketing and communication. Within a single minute at noon every day, there are over three thousand versions of our message that go out to customers, based on what they shop for, what they like, even what sizes they wear. It's tailored, one-to-one communication with the customer."[8] By hiring statisticians and data engineers who build creative algorithms and by pairing them with photography and copy teams, the Gilt Groupe is able to develop specific language and imagery that most appeals to each individual customer.

THE B2B CHALLENGE

The ultimate branding challenge for organizations today is this: If you are a business-to-consumer (B2C) product or service provider, such as Red Bull, Nordstrom, or Harley-Davidson, you have ample opportunity to communicate your brand impactfully. However, if you are a business-to-business (B2B) product or service provider, the toughest thing in the world is to control your brand's message since so many other people either have no idea what you do or tell the story of your brand based on their individual experience. Brands in the B2B space face a daunting predicament.

B2B brands, just like their B2C counterparts, have to communicate with prospects and customers who are much more empowered to discover everything they need to know about them independently. As a B2B brand, you are selling to the sold. The harder job is to sell a B2B brand to the people who don't know you. Marketo, a marketing automation company, tells its clients that 70 percent of the buying process in a complex sale is already complete before a potential customer is ready to engage with a salesperson. So how do B2B brands influence people who are on a discovery mission without them? The challenge varies company to company because in the technology business, for example, they already have the obstacle of explaining the complex, jargon-infused solutions in little time.

According to Kevin Randall, director of brand strategy and research at Movéo Integrated Branding, "brands matter because companies act just like people when it comes to evaluating what products or services to buy. Along with a number of explicit rational criteria, a powerful irrational impulse is always present to influence the purchase decision."[9]

Mohanbir Sawhney, professor of technology at the Kellogg School of Management at Northwestern University, suggests that B2B firms should focus their brand messaging on three areas:

1. Functional (what the product does)
2. Economic (what the brand means to the customer in time and money)
3. Emotional (how the brand makes the customer feel)[10]

"Brands that deliver beyond the functional and economic levels with emotional benefits will command an incremental price premium and create strong competitive advantage and customer brand loyalty," says Randall.[11] Cisco captured our imaginations in its "Human Network" campaign, taking its mundane router and showing us how it connects us to peers and other cultures around the world. Even software and software-as-a-service solutions can elicit an emotional response if the product brings the customer to the next level. Emotional connections lead to huge opportunities to take calculated risks to build and leverage your brand, but you need to have a CMO who understands how markets are shifting and how the CMO role is impacted in the process.

THE RISK FACTOR

Here's a case study of how one B2B company, NetApp, recognized that it was not a household name but worked to reestablish its identity. The data storage company aligned itself with *Forbes,* a brand that was synonymous with wealth and power.

Rebranding When You Are Not a Household Name

"Imagine your name is NetApp and you walk into a party. How would you introduce yourself? What would you say to impress everyone in the room?" asks a marketing manager at NetApp.[12] It is an exercise she experienced in a workshop that she has taken with her since. Within that moment, she recognized what her company needed to do to hook the executive target audience.

Founded in 1992, the company, originally called Network Appliance, became the leading data storage company and hit the revenue milestone of $1 billion during the Internet boom of the 1990s. Overcoming a dip after the burst of the tech bubble, the company's revenue has climbed steadily ever since and is over $6 billion today. NetApp, certainly not well-known for its data storage business outside of the tech world, wanted to have a voice on topics that its audience cared about. So, in 2009, the cofounder and the then-CMO, ran an assessment of the brand: She first asked the executive staff to describe what NetApp stood for. What she received in return was a generic presentation of words that painted a very nebulous picture, and she realized that NetApp had no real narrative or story. She went back and asked, "If NetApp were a person, who would it be?" But the executives found it hard to describe their brand in a "human-centric" manner. To unearth the company's real perception of its own brand, the marketing team then went through a discovery process. The aim was to derive the brand's persona, identity, and expression based on what the executive team believed the brand should stand for. Over the next 14 months, NetApp built a brand task force of more than 25 key internal stakeholders, including employees from marketing, sales, human resources, IT, and workplace resources. They worked through a large rebranding initiative and placed all the necessary levers to steer the organization in the new branding direction.

The result was an extensive visual and verbal brand transformation, including a new identity, name (shortened to NetApp), logo, messaging, architecture, and tone of voice. NetApp rebranded itself as the "friendly partner," with a tagline of "Go *further, faster.*" It

also focused on rebranding its logo so that the NetApp "N" would represent a gateway to more opportunities. An arch has significant meaning in matrimony, education, and history, but for NetApp, the arch symbolized a gateway to more opportunities, faster.

NetApp's efforts helped it move toward a much clearer brand identity, both to the outside world and internally. It is now associated with a more human touch and is also more tightly linked with its beloved culture. The change has given them more opportunities for recruiting talent, building stronger connections with customers, and exposure in the press.

In the past five years, NetApp's strategy has evolved to focus on serving larger enterprises, resulting in a need to refresh the company positioning, messaging, and brand platform. The company knew that its customers and partners had the notion that "There's something different about doing business with NetApp." To convert that thought into something more tangible for the company's new positioning, NetApp gathered feedback from more than 900 customers, partners, prospects, and internal leaders from around the world. The marketing team discovered that, in particular, customers value the vision that the NetApp team shares to help them make the best choices amid a complex IT landscape. The company plans to harness this thought for its new brand positioning, to be launched in late 2014.

How NetApp Aligned Its Brand to Another

Three years ago, NetApp marketing executives identified a confluence of media happenings. The previously distinct media types known in the industry as paid, earned, and owned media were beginning to converge into a melting pot of information that buyers could consume across many content sources. A buyer was becoming much more empowered by the multitude of channel options, ever-growing social networks, and plethora of mobile devices. "It used to be that a brand could rely on a great sales pitch to woo a prospect. During this earlier era, you could talk about yourself and your products until you eventually convinced the customer to buy something. Times were changing," said a marketing manager.[13]

What NetApp needed was a game plan that integrated its media strategy in order to have a greater influence on buyers. The company needed a game plan that would enable it to break through the increasingly noisy marketplace to gain mindshare.

So, the team set out to identify the best way to take advantage of this overlap. "We weren't looking for the traditional program, but rather an ability to build trust with customers by talking to them about what they care about, not what we care about. One of our first stops in search of a multimedia program was Forbes and a program called BrandVoice," said the marketing manager. According to the *Forbes* website, BrandVoice is an invitation-only, "innovative approach to integrating marketers' content with *Forbes*' editorial and users' content—allowing marketers to demonstrate their thought leadership on the *Forbes* platform using the same tools as content creators."[14] For NetApp, this program offered an opportunity to communicate directly to the enormous audience of executive readers on Forbes.com. The company was going to get a chance to talk to the *Forbes* audience, which is 70 percent C-suite, all of whom take great interest in technology, leadership, culture, partnerships, and customers. She admits, "What an opportunity! And what an intimidating task!"

Soon thereafter, executives of NetApp and Forbes started to have intimate conversations not just about media programs and marketing investments but also about business and economics. They wanted to figure out if the two would make a good marriage, so there was much discussion about NetApp's technology, its vision, and the ways in which its vision can improve business and society. The NetApp and Forbes executives talked about the value of culture and the mission of their respective businesses and discovered commonality. They discussed changing the business environment for the better, together. The two companies got to know each other, which generated trust and respect for each others' brand missions.

Over the next six months and about 100 conversations internally, NetApp took a test drive, working closely with Forbes to engage the executive audience and gain brand familiarity with a differentiated program that put NetApp in the driver's seat. On May 21, 2012, the company launched its BrandVoice platform on Forbes.com. Now in its second year, the program has provided the answer to what is top of mind for so many Fortune 500 CMOs: How do you improve brand health?

The NetApp marketing team believes that content marketing in the twenty-first century is about monetizing the most compelling forms of content and that NetApp should look to model itself along the lines of a traditional media outlet. They believe that media outlets seek to provide their audiences the best, most compelling news and information to create loyalty and brand equity. "Isn't that the same objective for most companies? Why wouldn't marketers approach content like a media outlet? Why wouldn't companies organize marketing teams like media houses?" they ask.

But to really sustain the fruits of these investments, the NetApp global communications team knew it had a few important things to fix. First, much of the compelling content that members created wasn't being leveraged. Second, the content that was being produced was guided by disparate goals, guidelines, and topics, which fueled brand inconsistency. Third, because the marketing team didn't have a common model by which to operate, many teams found it too hard to collaborate. They needed a further blueprint for success.

Tell Your Story in a Book

Through BrandVoice, members of the NetApp marketing team realized that content is what will help them win conversations about technology and business. In order to get deeper into these conversations, they needed content that's credible, authentic, compelling, and has lasting equity, so they set up a meeting with Rich Karlgaard, the publisher of *Forbes*, cofounder of the Churchill Club, and a 30-year veteran in the media business.

A small team and Karlgaard sat around a table and talked about an idea to write a business story. They all agreed that the biggest challenge was telling a credible business story that people would buy into. "Remember those discussions with Forbes about our mutual goals to impact business and leverage technology for economic success?" a marketing manager asked. "Well, Rich [Karlgaard] had been part of those discussions, so he quickly got it," she continued. They proposed that he author a book about the business virtues that develop when powerful companies find lasting success. They weren't interested in a corporate document about NetApp but a mainstream published book, so they reached out to the publishing house John Wiley & Sons. The result of this dialogue is Rich Karlgaard's book, *The Soft Edge: Where Great Companies Find Lasting Success*, which was published in April 2014.

NetApp's marketing team believes that the twin investments in BrandVoice and the Karlgaard book have tightly aligned NetApp with one of the most powerful media brands in business, *Forbes*. "We didn't let risk intimidate us, we didn't let our brand weaknesses get in our way, and we let our relentless ambition for customer success drive every aspect of the marketing approach to minimize risk and gain brand familiarity," says a manager on the marketing team.

Today, NetApp tells the branding/marketing story of how it changed the rules of the game. The marketing team members know that none of this could have happened without the NetApp culture. "I'm with team members who all stand united behind a powerful communication philosophy that promotes customer centricity, authenticity, fact-based data integrity, and knowledge share. Shouldn't that be what everyone believes in? Imagine what the information experience would be like for all of us if this were a common philosophy?" asks the senior manager.

CHAPTER TEN

The Era of Collaborative Sales and Customer Service

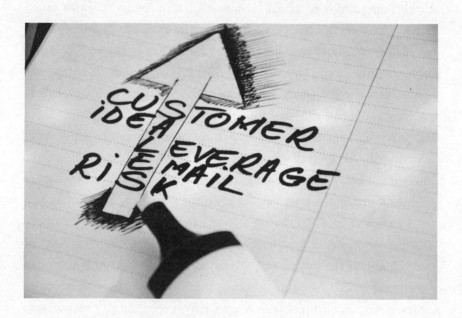

Norman Happ moved to Intuit, a leading provider of financial management and tax preparation software for small businesses and individuals, in November 2007, to direct sales of the small business division. (He has since become the vice president of Intuit's go-to-market division.) Previously he had founded two start-ups. "To have the freedom to experiment like an entrepreneur, but have the resources of an established company is part of the magic behind Intuit's growth," says Happ. The other component is Scott Cook's inspirational leadership, and his maniacal focus on a single mission: solving the needs of the customer.[1]

Cook founded Intuit in 1983, and though he could have left years ago and never worked again, like so many founders in Silicon Valley, he wants to watch the brainchild he gave birth to grow up. "One of the key distinctions about Scott is that he operates as a chief innovation officer and talent steward for innovators," says Happ. In practice, that means Cook is always deeply connected to the customer.

Intuit has two objectives: to do the nation's taxes and to handle the operations of small businesses. In order to do both effectively, Cook recognized that the company needed an approach to transform customer insights into products that customers love and can't imagine doing business without. His approach is comprised of two elements: customer-driven innovation and a design-thinking method called "Design for Delight." Intuit is always seeking a big unmet customer problem that it or its partners can solve well, which will also give the company a durable advantage. To do so, Intuit must know its customers so well that it can almost anticipate problems rather than waiting to hear of them through feedback.

Launched in 2007, Intuit's Design for Delight aims to evoke positive emotions in customers by exceeding their expectations at every point in the customer journey. It is composed of three principles and a set of design-thinking tools that embody those principles. They are: deep customer empathy, go broad to narrow, and rapid experimentation with customers. Several methods serve each principle.[2]

1. **Deep customer empathy** is visiting customers at their homes or places of work and studying them in their environments. Specific methods include using empathy maps and journey lines, a visual activity that helps Intuit staff understand their customers with all the strengths, weaknesses, skills, and

behaviors—the purpose being to better understand customers' experiences and expectations.[3]

2. **Go broad to narrow** involves Intuit staff using tools to ensure that they are exploring the full customer experience landscape before narrowing in on decisions. These tools include:

   a. **Brainstorming.** A process of ideation where a group gathers and comes up with multiple diverse ideas without judgment on the viability or correctness of the objective.

   b. **Brain-writing.** This is serial solo brainstorming in which one person writes down ideas in response to a challenge, hands the ideas to the next person, and then receives a third person's sheet with ideas and build on them. The objective is to constantly build on good ideas.

   c. **2 × 2 narrowing.** Selecting ideas based on the two most critical criteria. First, identify the criteria that are important to choosing an idea, select two criteria and map them out in two dimensions (e.g., vertical might be the criterion of size—big to small; horizontal might be speed—fast to slow), then map the ideas from the brainstorm to the two dimensions. Good ideas are the ones that fall into the quadrant of the two important criteria (e.g., big and fast).

   d. **Fact-opinion-guessing.** A method for mapping out knowledge, where you capture everything you think you know on individual sticky notes, post them, and cluster them into groups. Then for each sticky note, identify: facts (e.g., we have hard data on this), opinions (e.g., we have data that makes us think this is probably true), or guesses (e.g., we really don't know this but feel it's probably true). The team then identifies which opinions and guesses need to be converted to facts (what research needs to be done so they can ascertain hard data).

    e. **Affinity mapping.** Clustering things or ideas into groups to find patterns and meaningful relationships.

3. **Rapid experimentation** involves many of the methods heavily leveraged in lean methods described by Steve Blank and Eric Reis, who reignited the lean start-up movement. For example, the "Business Model Canvas" is about creating and experimenting with a minimum viable product and testing key assumptions.

Although Intuit launched Design for Delight as a way to streamline communications between sales and product managers, initially the program didn't catch on as anticipated. To help employees learn the methods associated with these principles, Intuit created a community of 200 "innovation catalysts" in September 2009 and directed specific employees who serve as coaches in various fields (such as HR, product managers, marketing directors, and customer care representatives) to spend up to 10 percent of their time training other teams in the Design for Delight methods. The catalysts cover four countries (the United States, United Kingdom, Canada, and India) and range from frontline employees to directors.

In early 2012, two innovation catalysts, Ben Blank and Aaron Eden, inspired after attending a Lean Start-up Weekend (a two-day, hands-on experience where entrepreneurs and aspiring entrepreneurs can find out if new ideas are viable), created a mechanism for bringing that format into Intuit. They invited teams across the company to participate in two-day "Lean Start-in" events. It was at one such event that Happ's story unfolded.

After assuming leadership of the sales organization within the small business division, Happ first tore the walls down between product developers and salespeople, so both would travel to customers and hear their needs firsthand. Second, Happ used Design for Delight, so that the sales organization could solve customers' problems quickly, in a way that evokes positive emotions in customers.

Happ recalled a time when he and the sales team were meeting in a conference room at the company's Tucson, Arizona, office. The team was baffled by flat sales of one of the company's products, QuickBooks Enterprise, which had been projected to grow revenues at 15 percent year over year, but fell far short. So Happ, along with an Intuit innovation catalyst and the rest of the sales executive team, dissected the product's offerings and discovered that customers were hesitant to purchase for two reasons: Quick-Books Enterprise required a license for five people, and the use of the word "enterprise" seemingly scared off small business owners, as the term is often associated with big enterprises.

Using Design for Delight methods, the team identified the opportunity to modify the product and the underlying assumptions that those modifications suggested. The key supposition was that if the licensure requirement was reduced from five people to one person, Intuit's best customers would be more likely to buy Quick-Books Enterprise. But was this true?

Immediately, Happ's team exited the conference room, went onto the sales floor, and got on the phone with 30 customers in the next hour to find out if reducing licensure to one person would solve the problem. Within 24 hours, the answer was a resounding yes. After making the changes to reduce the licensing requirement to one person (Intuit opted to maintain the word "enterprise"), QuickBooks Enterprise's revenue grew to 25 percent year over year and became 40 percent of QuickBooks' overall revenue.

When asked how to keep up with those revenue numbers, Happ responded, "Sales is always the pressure cooker, because you get a report card every day." Also, in the software-as-a-service world, you have to be incredibly agile, since material feature releases—significant new capabilities or user interface changes rolled out in the product itself (or website or whatever platform has the release)—occur every four weeks. The net positive for working at such a furious pace, according to Happ, is that "we're able to get fresh insights from our customers and apply them as close to real time as possible."

Traditional definition of sales	The act of selling a product or service in return for compensation.
Risk-taker's definition of sales	Being deeply dialed in to your customers' needs and having a sales force, product managers, and customer service reps who are focused on a human-centric approach.

ABANDONING THE SALES MACHINE

Sales used to be about blocking and tackling. It was pretty straight-forward: How many prospect calls did you make? How often did you recite the sales script? Did you use all of your closes before you walked away from the sale? Even with the development of methodologies that allow us to focus on systems to approach the complex interaction between a sales representative and customer, the sales process, long called the sales machine, is no longer performing as intended. Why? For three central reasons.

First, one of the hardest things about selling today is that customers don't need salespeople the way they used to. When buyers were less knowledgeable, they relied on sales reps to inform them of the features and benefits of products. But now, with the nearly infinite amount of information available to us instantly through the Internet, buyers can balance the scales. Companies are employing sophisticated buying teams and purchasing consultants, easily defining solutions for themselves.

Second, anyone associated with sales is aware of the quota-oriented strategy, and in today's human-centric world, it no longer resonates. Most companies hire, train, compensate, and manage their sales teams differently from the rest of the company. Much of this difference is based on the premise that salespeople are driven by money and individual achievements, always in competition with other salespeople both inside and outside of the company. These sales professionals have to meet objectives within strict time frames by placing demanding priorities on transactional activities that generate income. Although this may be fine for driving short-term growth, it doesn't necessarily foster sustainable long-term sales or trusting relationships with customers.

The Corporate Executive Board (CEB), a leading member-based advisory company, states that sales performance is growing increasingly ineffectual, with companies reporting longer sales cycle times, lower conversion rates, less reliable forecasts, and compressed margins. In a November 2013 *Harvard Business Review* article, "Dismantling the Sales Machine," Brent Adamson, Matthew Dixon, and Nicholas Toman of the CEB determined that new sales approaches are "built to outsell less focused, less disciplined competitors through brute efficiency and world-class tools and training."[4] In other words, progressive sales approaches create a new breed of competitors, who also are trained in modern sales methodologies, which ultimately makes traditional salespeople both unproductive and overprocessed in inauthentic verbiage—approaches that run counter to being human-centric.

Finally, the problem with the quota-oriented strategy is that a majority of salespeople have a long and less-than-distinguished history of becoming nearly invisible as soon as the ink dries and monies are committed. Companies encourage this by compensating sales professionals more for winning deals than for ensuring that customers are happy and satisfied.

So, then what? Then, there is customer service.

WHAT CUSTOMER SERVICE? DO YOU NO LONGER LOVE ME?

Customers are increasingly frustrated with the level of services they experience:

- *91 percent [of] respondents are frustrated that they have to contact a company multiple times for the same reason;*
- *90 percent for being put on hold for a long time;*

- *89 percent by having to repeat their issue to multiple representatives.*
- *Globally, there is a 4 percent increase in switching due to poor customer service, from 62% to 66%.*

—2013 Accenture Global Consumer Pulse Survey

We've all been there. What is going on with customer service is anyone's guess, but the lack of customer service, which started in the airline and technology industries—industries that could once afford to piss off customers—can no longer get away with bad behaviors because it has finally had an impact on the bottom line.

Dennis Snow, the author of *Unleashing Excellence: The Complete Guide to Ultimate Customer Service,* a renowned public speaker on customer service, and a former manager of the Disney Institute and Disney University, believes that customer service lost its way after three things happened.[5] First, companies put all their focus and resources on the product rather than on the experience of the product; in other words, the product became the only thing that mattered. Second, some companies believed (and still do) that the only thing that's important is price, the lowest price, so they put all of their efforts into making their price the lowest, sacrificing ongoing service in order to maintain margin. Kmart is pretty much going out of business because of poor customer experience, in spite of low prices. This strategy worked well for Walmart for some time, but Amazon is now going to take a good chunk out of Walmart's market share because it offers low prices and great customer service. A good proof point of the low-cost, customer service takeover is that of Southwest Airlines—the company repudiates the industry's lousy customer service record and is one of the few profitable airlines. Third, it takes effort to build a customer service culture and get buy-in from senior management and throughout the organization. Doing so entails understanding what customers want, hiring the right employees, plus ongoing service training and communication, measurement, and accountability. At a bare minimum, it is a three- to five-year process. Snow says the problem is that most executives ask him, "If I do exactly what you tell me, what will the net be to my bottom line?" His unswerving retort has been and continues to be this: "I can't provide a one-to-one correlation because so many factors impact the bottom line. But all of the evidence validates that the quality of the customer experience, good or bad, impacts the bottom line."

There is irrefutable evidence that good customer service increases the bottom line. Jim Cramer, host of the CNBC show *Mad Money,* demonstrated how the stocks of 17 companies that have mastered the art of customer service (e.g., Whole Foods, Amazon, Apple, Southwest, and Nordstrom) beat out the rest of the market with a Standard & Poor's 257 percent return versus the rest of the S&P return of 65 percent.[6]

A study conducted by BIGResearch for the National Retail Federation and American Express "found that 85 percent of consumers shop more often and spend more at retailers that offer higher levels of customer service." The same research also found that "82 percent said that they are likely to recommend retailers with superior customer service to friends and family."[7] Snow says, "The net is far greater to long-term loyalty than what my clients look for in the immediate bottom line." Companies must look at the long-term net effect of customer loyalty, driven by great customer experiences, has on their bottom line. We've all heard the saying "It's cheaper to keep a current customer than it is to attract a new one." It turns out that positive customer experiences not only help us to keep current customers, it also turns those customers into a terrific sales force for the company.

Customer service has gotten so bad that people are choosing no service over bad customer service, insists Snow. "People are willing to buy a set of Skull Candy earphones at a premium price out of a Best Buy kiosk at the airport rather than deal with going into a physical Best Buy." Self-service has become customary at grocery stores. It seems that an increasing number of consumers are willing to spend hundreds of dollars buying something from a vending machine rather than having to interact with uncaring employees. With customer expectations so low, those companies with employees who are simply friendly, knowledgeable, and efficient are a welcome relief to weary buyers. Snow tells his clients that customer expectations today are really minimal, but they do have an interest in speed and convenience, which is why companies such as Amazon, Zappos, and Nordstrom, among others, will win big time. "It is such a simple formula: know what you're doing, do it efficiently, and be nice to me while you're doing it," says Snow.

MARRYING CUSTOMER SERVICE: "WILL THY CUSTOMER SERVICE TAKE THY SALES?"

Snow is absolutely convinced that his best customer service expertise came from when he started his Disney career on the frontline, working the park's attractions. "We learned that Walt Disney World isn't selling rides and shows; we [the entertainment company] were selling an experience," says Snow. And Disney stressed that its cast members (employees) are an integral part of that experience. Disney takes this concept so seriously that all leaders are expected to work a frontline shift at least twice a year in order to stay connected to what's really important to the organization's success. Through these experiences, management can learn more about what's working and not working rather than reading any report. "I tell my [executive] clients today that if they really want to know their customers' pain points, spend a half day at your call center, and listen in on what your customers think about your company," says Snow.

A former client told Snow about a workshop he had conducted for a group of salespeople that was also attended by the customer service department. One of the salespeople stated, "Hey, we sell the dream." One of the customer service people responded, "Yeah, and we service the nightmare." According to Snow, in today's market, you can't be thinking that you can rely on a single sale anymore. A sales team's success relies on share of wallet and referrals and is much more about the overall experience, so the only way to effectively sell in this era of collaboration is if the customer sees the sales and service practice as one.

World-class organizations are constantly studying their customers, not by surveys but by really observing their customers in the moment, so they can make determinations on what the customers' thresholds and expectations are. Disney has figured out how to commoditize the experiential differentiator by deeply dialing in to what exasperates customers and then doing something about it. The frustration of waiting in line has always been top of mind for Disney executives, and a succession of steps have been taken to address this problem—from wait time signs, entertainment in the lines, make the line part of the experience, and FastPass (fast entry with no waiting in line), all of which address the pain points. Now the company has addressed this pain point at a new generational level: FastPass+ allows park visitors to make a reservation for their favorite attraction from their home.

THE RISK FACTOR

The goal of this chapter is to demonstrate the expansion of mindset that occurs when companies think about the sales function in this new era of collaboration. Intuit integrates engineers not only to solve customers' needs quickly but to anticipate them. Disney and Apple provide experiential customer service experiences. Here's how you can design a fresh sales climate.

Explore Talent Outside of Sales

Based on data CEB collected on more than 4 million professionals around the world, only 17 percent of existing sales employees score high on the competencies required for success in insight selling. The sales labor market still skews strongly toward emotional intelligence rather than IQ. In order to succeed in this climate, managers will have to reconsider the way they hire sales professionals by focusing on individuals, possibly with no background in sales, who have exceptional critical thinking skills.

Recall our discussion of IDEO and the hiring of T-shaped people in The Death of HR and the Birth of Talented People chapter, deep expertise in one area and a broad interest in many fields. These people are the most valuable cross-pollinators—individuals who see patterns others don't and apply key differences to new contexts. These individuals look beyond current challenges and tackle a problem by considering solutions beyond the obvious or standard concept. Similarly, sales organizations need to seek individuals with deep expertise in one area and who embody an array of other experiences.

To attract and retain nontraditional hires for sales roles, managers should make clear that their employment value resides in their ability to support individual decision-making and emphasize the importance of collaboration and judgment. Also, managers must shift the emphasis from extrinsic, short-term rewards, such as higher variable compensation, to intrinsic, long-term motivators, such as autonomy and the opportunity to generate value for customers. CEB's research proves that "building a climate with the right incentives and rewards can boost the effort that salespeople make above and beyond their basic job requirements by 10% and increase their intent to stay by more than 30%."[8]

Selling without Salespeople

In the relatively new area of selling without salespeople, consultants or engineers who are already embedded within client activities assess additional needs and present possible solutions to clients. Everyone should be incentivized to sell—including product developers, finance people, branding and marketing staff—anyone who meets with and listens closely to the needs of potential clients. In both cases, bringing product experts to the conversation helps not only to answer clients' functional needs and address possible problems in advance but assists with the emotional side of the buying process, by having clients meet and work closely with the people who are building the product or delivering the service.

Customers as Collaborators

We have seen the power of client referral. Financial advisors, for example, live and die by a consistent flow of referrals from happy customers. So why don't we take this to the next level? Bring your customers into the sales process and find ways to compensate them (either individually or company-wide) for helping sell to new clients. I am not talking about the old Amway or other pyramid selling methods. This is more about building partnerships with your customers, who can provide customer-oriented perspectives that inside sales can't necessarily anticipate or replicate. It is an acknowledgment that both parties are responsible for working together to find all of the information needed to solve a problem, sell the solution, and reap the benefits. This method allows you to take trust-based risk to explore all alternatives to meeting other customer's needs.

Human-Centric Teams

To succeed in this new collaborative sales environment, as I mentioned earlier, sales leaders must deemphasize their traditional selling processes and embrace a flexible approach to selling, an approach driven by making customers partners in the process, by improvising to deliver value, and by seeking out broader perspectives to help provide insight. The human-centric sales force is there not only to solve problems but to anticipate them. You need to be so tuned in to your customers' pain points that you feel their pain and elicit genuine emotion in customer responses. Because no two customers are alike, you need to be nimble and intrinsically risk tolerant.

Then you have to be collaborative with your team. Even within the most effective sales teams, the individual is no longer as valuable to the bottom line as the whole group. For instance, a large media company that invested in an internal social networking platform to help generate leads found that cross-sales increased, cycle times declined, and conversion rates went up. By working collaboratively, one sales account drove $3.5 million in incremental revenue.[9] "Social media is fast becoming a major asset for customer-facing teams across entire organizations, from sales to customer support. Businesses are really starting to see the benefits of using social media to enhance customer engagement and reap the benefits of social selling," says Gregory Gunn, vice president of business development at HootSuite, the social media dashboard company.[10] Gunn believes that social media in the team environment helps cultivate relationships with customers far faster, closing deals far easier than past sales approaches.

Whether it is through social media or relationship-driven sales, by emphasizing human-centric sales teams, managers can create demand earlier in the sales funnel rather than responding to it later. To do this, managers should give reps greater latitude in the qualification, prioritization, and pursuit of individual opportunities, recognizing that reps are more likely to succeed when they feel supported rather than held accountable for those outcomes, especially unreasonable ones.

As discussed in chapter 1 regarding jazz ensembles, sales organizations built as supportive teams actually allow for better risk-taking and a fuller, more complete experience. Improvement is accelerated through the sharing and testing of ideas via peer interaction. Imagine how effective you will be in closing deals if you have a team who can improvise the sales process based on the customer, using strengths of some to cover weaknesses of others.[11]

This fits the modern view of customer expectations, as customers want partners they collaborate with and products they can trust. The key is to give salespeople considerable discretion to improvise and take risks while guiding them through—and holding them accountable for—specific milestones, such as building a trusting relationship with customers on the way to sales.

Hire the New Empathetic Salesperson

Sales professionals are relationship experts, problem solvers, knowledge facilitators, therapists, innovators, and so much more. The new salesperson needs to be more of a knowledge worker, someone who is entrusted with executing company strategy and defining the organization's value to the customer. Increasingly, the best salespeople exhibit the same attributes seen in any great leader:

- Listener
- Empathizer
- Collaborative problem-solver
- Trustworthy
- Communicator
- Strategizer
- Improviser
- Facilitator
- Calculated risk-taker

Change the Compensation Model

Business-to-customer sales have had to change drastically, especially on high-ticket items, such as automobile sales and real estate. In a *Wall Street Journal* article titled "Say Goodbye to the Car Salesman," the AutoTrader Group reported that "the average car shopper spends more than 11 hours online researching cars and only 3-½ hours offline, including trips to the dealership."[12] With that amount of information researched, it has become harder to reward salespersons for charging higher prices. In fact, many car dealerships are cutting commissions altogether and offering no-haggle pricing that more closely reflect Internet prices. Dealerships are increasingly hiring people who are adept with both computers and customer relationships.

In the world of real estate, no practice has been more difficult to change than that of calculating sales agents' commissions. Then

along came a maverick by the name of Ken DeLeon of DeLeon
Realty in Palo Alto, California. A former trademark and patent
lawyer at the Silicon Valley law firm Wilson Sonsini Goodrich &
Rosati, DeLeon knew that anything in Silicon Valley could be improved, even the way real estate had been marketed, bought, and
sold. DeLeon believes that the traditional approach of paying an
agent a commission based on how much a buyer pays for a house
misaligns incentives. "Your agent should not make more money
because you agreed to pay more or earn less because they told you
not to put in an offer based on problems in the inspection reports,"
states DeLeon.[13] Rather than paying agents commissions, DeLeon
claims that he pays his agents exceptional salaries in addition to
full benefits and matched 401(k) contributions.

Build Memories for Your Customers

Over the years, NetApp had taken the time to get to know the personalities and interests of its best and potential customers.

In the fall of 2013, the NetApp Sponsored News team met
to discuss new approaches for one of the toughest sales quarters. The goal was to engage customers in conversations about
data, culture, and technology decisions. Inspired by this notion of
powerful pairs, the team came up with the idea of a weekend get-
away around the shared passion of some customers: race cars and
technology. As I stated in the Corporate Culture of How chapter, at the time, Formula One was coming to Austin, Texas—its
second year in the United States—and the Sauber Formula One
racing team happened to be a NetApp customer. Someone on the
marketing team said, "What if NetApp marketing could get the
Sauber racing team to give our best customers a personal tour of
the NetApp technology that Sauber uses for its Formula One cars
and create a memorable experience?"

On November 15, 2013, NetApp invited its best customers to
gather in Austin for what some described as "a once-in-a-lifetime
opportunity." The customers and a few NetApp executives met

with Sauber racecar drivers, engineers, and executives to learn the ins and outs of what it takes to be a Formula One racing team on the world circuit. NetApp did so without putting on the heavy sales pitch. In fact, noticeably absent from the event was anyone from the sales force except for the executive vice president of Channel Sales for the Americas. "It was a no-pressure experience, focused on building stronger relationships and trust with our customers," says NetApp's marketing head of this event.[14]

In fact, one of the attendees was so taken by his experience at Formula One, he wanted to keep in touch with the rest of the NetApp customers he met. "[One customer] came to us and said can you set up a NetApp community so we can all stay in touch with one another?" the marketing head explained. "It was rewarding to see our customers wanting to continue to engage with one another. . . . I guess we created a sense of community and perhaps a memory for life."

Customer Service Narrative

Who doesn't know about Nordstrom's exceptional customer service? (Nordstrom is well-known for taking back just about any product at any time, with or without a receipt.) One of the ways that Nordstrom reinforces its customer service culture to its over 60,000 employees is through the following narrative, based on a real story that happened many years ago:

> A woman in Alaska enters into a Nordstrom with a set of faulty tires and attempts to return it to the salesperson behind the counter. The saleswoman is perplexed, as Nordstrom is a clothing retailer, but the customer insists that she bought the tires at that location and demands her money back. The salesperson could have refused the return—after all, the tires had been purchased from a tire company—but the Nordstrom store manager gladly refunded her money, and the customer walked away satisfied.

Of course, Nordstrom never sold tires but, in 1975, it purchased four buildings from a company that did, Northern Commercial of Alaska. Why do Nordstrom executives share this story with every new permanent, part-time, and holiday employee? Because it is a story that precisely embodies the Nordstrom culture. Instead of listing some monotonous and meaningless mission statement, such as "We Stand for Customer Service," executives share who they are, what they represent, what their values are in a story that can be told, retold, and recollected. Amy Jones, VP of corporate affairs at Nordstrom and responding on behalf of Blake Nordstrom, the current CEO and a fourth-generation Nordstrom, wrote in an email: "The story illustrates our belief that offering customers the best possible shopping experience is the best thing we can do to earn their business now and in the future. While the customer's definition of service has evolved with the many shopping channels and technologies available today, staying relevant means we need to meet their expectations no matter how they want to shop with us."[15]

Experiential Customer Service

We think of Apple as the world's leading innovator of products, yet we overlook that it is a leader in exceptional customer service as well. From an experiential customer service standpoint, Apple gets you involved in the practice. According to Dennis Snow, every Apple employee is highly knowledgeable and enthusiastic about the products. Employees do three things really well to make customers feel like a partner in the process:

1. They quickly gauge how tech savvy the customer is and seamlessly adjust their approach.
2. When a purchase is made that will require in-store configuration, they ask the customer to open the product's box, because it's part of the Apple experience.
3. They are always willing to help.

Snow recalled a time that he brought in an iPad that he was having some problems with. The employee made him feel that he was the most important customer in the store, even though that visit wasn't going to result in a sale. But, for Snow, that one experience resulted in many, many sales since.

CONCLUSION

"Yes, and . . . ?"

A ship is always safe at the shore—but that is NOT what it is built for.

— Albert Einstein

Early on in my career, an up-and-coming lawyer who despised the billable hour asked me, "What's the worst thing that can happen if you stand up and do the right thing?" I shrugged my shoulders. Eager to answer his own question, he responded, "You get fired."

It is easier to get fired when you are a 20-something, have no mortgage, and no other mouths to feed, but this person's advice stuck with me throughout my life. I have done the right thing—reliably—and have been, in fact, fired for it.

I was thrown onto a political land mine over a very heated social policy issue: neighborhood schools and the busing of school-children. As the lobbyist for a school system in Charlotte, North Carolina (the only lobbyist job I ever had), two people were emphatic that I act on their behalf—the school superintendent and the chair of the school board. In some ways, both of them were my bosses, but only one had hiring and firing power over me. While they were on the same side of the issue that supported the busing of schoolchildren, their approaches on how I should perform my job were vastly different. I was hired to kill a piece of legislation.

Two men simultaneously ran for the North Carolina General Assembly—one in the House and one in the Senate—on this very issue and, once elected, introduced a bill to ban busing schoolchil-dren in Charlotte in both the House and Senate. Their aim was to see which bill they could move through faster. If one failed, they still had the corresponding bill in the other legislative body. The men supported neighborhood schools because they had moved to new housing developments specifically to have their children at-tend schools within walking distance of their homes. Now they were facing their own children being bused out of the neighbor-hood to achieve greater racial balance at another school. This was particularly sensitive to this school district since Charlotte was the birthplace of the school busing issue. In 1971, *Swann v. Charlotte-Mecklenburg Board of Education* was brought before the U.S. Supreme Court, which ruled that busing could play a role in the continued desegregation in order to strive for greater racial balance in schools.

I had become emotionally invested in the issue and took a risk to try to win any vote to kill the bill in the House, thinking that I was doing the right thing. So much tension surrounded the impend-ing vote that journalists from local papers and regional magazines followed almost every move I made (what ensued I still hope to document in a political thriller one day—loosely based on this experience, of course).

Anyone knowledgeable about politics in the South will appreciate what I faced: notes slipped under my hotel room door late at night, requests for meetings in dark places, and threats that I won't go into here. In the end, we lost (failing to kill the bill) by one vote. A backroom deal had been made with the Speaker of the House that if the vote resulted in a tie (which it did) the Speaker would cast his vote in favor of the bill.

Shortly thereafter, I was fired by the school superintendent, who felt that the school board chairman had had too much influence in how I got things done. In essence, I was the fall guy for a deal that didn't go as planned. One magazine wrote an in-depth exposé of why I was—unjustly—fired. In the article, the very two legislators I fought so hard against talked about their respect for the job I had done. I was 28 years old. I took a risk, and while the outcome may have been painful in the moment—losing both the battle and my job—I was able to sleep at night.

NOTHING GREAT COMES FROM PLAYING IT SAFE

It is hard to take risks because we fear the unknown. Our minds run wild with questions like: What will happen once I risk something? If I take the risk, and it doesn't work out, what do I sacrifice? How do I recover? What happens if I don't take the risk? Can I live with the regret, a missed opportunity, the chance to define my relevance? We feel vulnerable, because we know that we can either win big or lose it all. And sometimes that risk can direct who we become as a person. It's human nature. However much we might wish otherwise, people are social animals. We care about what other people think, and every time we make a decision, we invite judgment. Our possessions and wealth, our friends and family, our career—any of these can take a hit if we're wrong. When we do risk right, we just might find something great on the other end.

There is risk in taking risk, and our discomfort with it is entirely natural. But that doesn't mean overcoming our vulnerability and getting into the practice of taking risk is not worthwhile.

On one of my overseas sabbaticals, I met a German woman in a bar in Granada, Nicaragua. We were deep in conversation about American culture, which I have found to be a favorite subject of expats and global travelers who favor touring the Third World. In her heavy German accent, she said to me, "You Americans are so consumed with your rules . . . marriage by 30 . . . 2.5 kids . . . and a picket fence. . . . It is no wonder you all have to visit a therapist every time you don't rise to your expectations." At first, her bluntness stunned me, but when I really thought about it, I blurted out, "I see your point."

Although the woman was speaking of American *social* culture, I think her comments apply to most business cultures as well. At work, we are boxed in by so many rules and expectations that if we deviate the least bit, we are outcasts, even liabilities. Even entrepreneurs, who are more daring at first, encounter more guidelines once venture capital enters the picture. Large organizations, which are built to exploit economies of scale, fall victim to fighting to "protect" the status quo, the norm, all leading to unmemorable results. The downside for these big companies is now so massive that they hire professionals just to minimize the vulnerabilities. Again, so much of the role of the HR professional is to bring abnormal behavior to the normal. Risk aversion has become the golden rule.

Then there is the income statement. Revenues and expenses tell "the story," which is why risk has been managed primarily by the finance department. Leaders must perform the ultimate of modern balancing acts by maintaining current business while also winning future business and managing innovation without negatively impacting the income statement. Hence, income statements are the primary barometer of how an organization is actually performing, a measure of its tangible value.

But what if we also measure *intangible* value? What if we take into account the hearts and minds of our talent? If we could put a figure on the value of our culture, with its ability to move fast, create new ideas, even change the world, would leaders and investors act differently? Would we finally start training our people in the finer skills of advanced risk-taking? Would our business schools start teaching it to our future leaders? It is happening, but not fast enough to save many companies from extinction due to excessive caution.

It is the leader's job to make risk-taking a foundational part of the company culture before competitors do. All production work should be geared toward getting better, faster, and stronger, which can't be accomplished without trying new things. The more employees are involved, the more skilled they are, the more diverse their roles within the company, the more effective the results.

Often these commitments to better, faster, and stronger are seemingly impossible to achieve. Many times these pressure cooker expectations translate into meeting if not exceeding top-line sales to drive bottom-line results. Those line items in the middle that may be innovative or groundbreaking, or could provide a new area of competitive advantage, get reduced or just plain removed. Some of these items may get pushed to the next reporting period, and the next, and the next, ultimately going away forever. In other words, the risk-taking required to enable innovation gets jettisoned and the trite and true remains, even if the company faces a shrinking market share. The innovative product that will require the acquisition of new and additional talent (increased headcount) with skills that currently don't exist in the organization just won't happen. Why? Because hiring will add unplanned cost and impact that manager's profit and loss statement and, ultimately the business's income statement.

I understand the challenge, but are we not putting a disproportionate focus on the challenges and not enough on the opportunities—the opportunities to bring the company into the next generation, to do the right thing, to lead or dramatically alter our industries, to fully embrace all of our talent and the talent of others?

How do we begin to put risk-taking in place? The next section presents a set of questions that can help unleash bold character leadership and provide a process for establishing a risk-taking company culture.

THE RISK FACTOR ASSESSMENT

1. **Assess your risk-taking style.**
   - How do you determine when is the optimal time to take risk?
   - How do you accelerate your knowledge about the risk you are about to take?
   - What do you gain or lose with a single decision?
   - When do you give up on an idea you have been pursuing?
   - Whom do you find to mentor you on the bigger risk-taking?

2. **Know your organization.**
   - What risks were taken, and paid off, over the last three years? Who took them, and how?
   - During the same period, which risks failed? How do the risk-taking successes and failures differ, and what do they have in common?
   - Throughout the company's history, what pivotal risks got it to where it is today?
   - Which positions inherently call for more risk-taking? Which require less?
   - Which rules governing risk might be for the comfort of managers rather than in the best interests of the company? Which rules could be eliminated, and which are critical?

3. **Know your people (including directors, shareholders, and the executive leadership team).**
   - Who's a risk-taker, and who is risk-averse?
   - In general, where does each person fall on the Risk Continuum—more toward behaviors that are static or chaotic, or somewhere in between? (See the discussion in The DNA of a Bold Risk-Taker chapter).

- Regarding the actions of others, when do they lean toward control? When do they allow for more freedom?
- What special skills and interests do your employees have? Are they hobbyists with a special skill? What are they passionate about? Have you utilized these in the business?
- Do you allow everyone the opportunity to be innovative? If so, how?

4. **Establish risk-taking parameters.**
   - Which type of risk do you reward the most? Which do you penalize?
   - Do people have permission to fail?
   - What wounds do you have that may prevent you from wanting to take risk? What stops others from being vulnerable enough to take risks?

5. **Know your processes.**
   - Do you have a formal innovation process in place that includes the whole organization, such as improvisational innovation (refer to the Improvisational Innovation chapter)?
   - What structures are in place to encourage and reward idea development?
   - How do you green-light ideas?
   - Under what circumstances might your managers kill ideas?
   - How do you get ideas from your less outgoing people?
   - How do you catalog ideas and their results?

6. **Know your knowledge base.**
   - What do your people know well? What don't they know?
   - How much time does it take to learn an advanced job or gain auxiliary skills in the average position in your company?
   - How do people communicate what they know, or want to know, with others?
   - How are your employees encouraged to learn other parts of the business? What do your customers or other stakeholders do?

- How do you learn about the business problems and concerns of others?
- How does your organization source your talents and record knowledge? How does it disseminate this base of knowledge to others exactly when it is needed?
- How have you enabled knowledge advisors and mentors to help others?

7. **Know the types of risk and the behaviors that support them.**
   a. Improvisational risk
      - Do you respond to ideas with "Yes, and . . . ?" as discussed throughout this book?
      - Do you listen without judgment?
      - Do you support and listen closely to others while they are taking risk?
      - Do you have a goal in mind?
      - Are you honest when a risk has lost momentum or didn't quite turn out as expected? Do others step in to help mitigate and recover from the unsuccessful risk?
      - Have you redefined the definition of failure? Are you public about supporting project outcomes and the people behind them when projects don't work as planned?
   b. Operational risk
      - How do you assess what can be improved?
      - How do you provoke ideas for improvement?
      - How do you prove that improvement can be made?

THE POWER OF "YES, AND . . . ?"

Of all my books, this one has been the most enthralling to reflect on for two pivotal reasons. First, I am captivated by risk-takers—truly fascinated by what makes them tick, how they balance out their immense passions with the sometimes mundane day-to-day responsibilities of family life, and whether they can make it all work. (I have found that many great risk-takers end up divorced.)

To have the opportunity to meet, interview, and be inspired by some of the world's greatest risk-takers has been one of the decisive gifts of my professional career. Second, this book gave me a chance to further reflect on the two very dichotomous cultures in which I have spent my career—Washington, DC, and Silicon Valley. In my opinion, it is an important case study to diagnose how the environment—or the mind-set of its people—can very deeply influence who you are and who you will become; one's milieu has the ability to direct your entire life.

In *Secrets of Silicon Valley,* I wrote about when my husband and I first moved to Silicon Valley in 2006. At the time, I would be standing in line at Starbucks, grocery stores, or the bank, and random people would just talk to me. They'd learn a bit of my story and immediately ask, "How can I help you? Whom can I introduce you to?" In no time, I was being introduced to some of Silicon Valley's most powerful entrepreneurs, venture capitalists, angel investors, and lawyers. It still happens today. Business outsiders who come to Silicon Valley are surprised by how affable and proactive people are in Silicon Valley. This culture is an anomaly. Many people believe it can be found only in the Valley and is difficult to replicate elsewhere.

What I later realized was that "How can I help you? Who can I introduce you to?" was just the beginning. What unfolded from there was the phrase "Yes, and . . . ?" Sometimes I would hesitantly share an idea that I had or I'd make a recommendation to a company that I advise, and the response would be "Yes, and . . .?" No one said, "No," or "Yes, but . . . ," throwing up potential roadblocks to my ideas. It was as if getting to that first base was a given, so I should already be thinking about what would come next.

What took me so long to recognize was what life can be like without the negativity and shallow egotism that I had been accustomed to in Washington, DC. Why wasn't anyone shooting me down? Why wasn't anyone squashing my enthusiasm or telling me that my idea is stupid or that it has already been done? (My favorite East Coast response when I would share an idea is, "Well, if it is so easy, then someone else would have already done it.")

There is a distinct reason why Silicon Valley has had since its birth—and continues to have—so much success. It is its culture, and the Silicon Valley mind-set is something that everyone should strive to adopt. It is a mind-set of meritocracy, where anyone at any time can put forth a great idea and be heard. It is a mind-set that doesn't care who you are, where you came from, what neighborhood you live in, what car you drive. It cares about your value. In this climate, it's so much easier to close your eyes and jump.

Imagine what we could all achieve if we just changed our perspective and adopted more of the Silicon Valley risk-taking mind-set, if we walked away from the script we have known for so long and improvised in a way that encourages people, not discourages them.

Imagine what the world could look like if we all walked around hearing and saying, "Yes, and . . . ?" Not worrying about what anyone thinks. Believing in ourselves—trusting ourselves—and pushing forward. More of us would feel encouraged and inspire others to be bold and audacious risk-takers. In the words of one of the world's greatest risk-takers of all time, which appeared in a 1997 Apple advertisement, Steve Jobs states:

> Here's to the crazy ones. The misfits. The rebels. The troublemakers. The round pegs in the square holes.
>
> The ones who see things differently. They're not fond of rules. . . . You can quote them, disagree with them, glorify or vilify them.
>
> But the only thing you can't do is ignore them. Because they change things. . . . They push the human race forward.
>
> Maybe they have to be crazy. . . .
>
> While some see them as the crazy ones, we see genius. Because the people who are crazy enough to think they can change the world, are the ones who do.[1]

Acknowledgments

Writing a book is always an arduous process. It is a journey that forces you to explore yourself, for better or worse. It is mental, emotional and physical. To this day, writing a book is—by far—the hardest thing that I have accomplished professionally. You always feel some degree of vulnerability when you put forth a book with bold new thinking.

There were three events that were largely responsible for setting the tone of this book.

First, just prior to signing the contract, my husband, Dino, said to me—insisting that he meant it in the most complimentary way possible—"You can be the funniest person in the room or the boldest badass . . . make sure this book reflects that." (*For the purposes of keeping the book clean, I may have cleaned his language up a bit.*)

Second, David Rose, chair of the New York Angels, once said at Singularity University in Mountain View, "Everything you know to be true, is not." In essence, just because we have been doing something a certain way forever doesn't mean it is the only right way. His words have always stuck with me.

Third, my then eight-year-old son, Dominick, would wake up and pepper me with questions continuously throughout the day about why this . . . why that, as it relates to physics and other scientific wonders. "What would happen if earth fell out of its gravity force?" he would ask. Thanks to Neil deGrasse Tyson, I have a fairly hobbyist knowledge of what would happen if the earth was off its axis. Without going too deep into my response, I said, "Everything would spin on its head."

Blend these three events together, and I found my relevance to put forth a definition of risk:

Vulnerability + Funny + Bold + "Everything you know to be true, is not" + Everything will spin on its head = Risk

I am a bold risk-taker, always have been, but I do it with humor, including plenty of laughing at myself. I am one of those people who has never been able to accept things as they are, always visualizing a better way, a better design, a brighter color. But today, most of what I do is driven by principle, to right an injustice, especially when it comes to human or civil rights.

In the journey of writing this book, I learned that the best way to mitigate risk is to surround yourself with the most brilliant thinkers. With that in mind, I took this journey with many talented people, but none more valuable than my speaking agent, Michael Humphrey, who, I detected very early on, is extremely gifted in intellect and spends most of his days talking to companies about the problems he needs to help solve. Mike and I held daily court about what is wrong and right with the organization of business, especially in relation to how people are treated. While he continued to talk to corporations and shared with me what he was hearing, I took a deep dive at a select few companies, most notably NetApp, where I spent over a year walking its hallways to really figure out why people loved working there so much.

NetApp

The person at NetApp that I have to thank from the bottom of my heart is Annalisa Camarillo. Without her, this book would not be what it is. Annalisa, who works at NetApp as a global branding and communication senior manager, saw me speak at the Churchill Club in April 2013 at the launch of my last book and reached out to have lunch to talk about collaborating on something—it became this book. It has been an extraordinary journey. Worthy of equal gratitude is Anjali Acharya, who shepherded and facilitated most every detail with such grace. Thank you to NetApp's CEO, Tom Georgens, for meeting with me and inspiring me with some of my best work. Other notable NetApp employees include, but are not limited to, Valentin Bercovici, Julie Parrish, and Jessica Rose.

IDEO

I've gotten to know so many wonderful people at IDEO. Most notably, Dave Blakely, with whom I gathered on a semi-regular basis to talk about theories around innovation. We later realized that we were great collaborators, so I ended up teaming up with Dave and IDEO to work on innovation process. I had a great conversation with David Rudman about the importance of people and talent development and am always charmed by Vicki Dalrymple, who would bug me about getting back to IDEO. Vicki is always wanting to know what my kids are up to, and in the process trying to feed me enticing candy on her desk.

Qualcomm

Thank you to Paul Jacobs, Navrina Singh, Catherine Baker, and Kathrin Rusert, who entrusted me with as much as I could learn about Qualcomm's innovation process. A debt of gratitude goes to Joseph Schuman, in Qualcomm's public affairs office, who helped shape my thinking of the importance of protecting the inventor.

There are countless people to thank for all their support. I want to call out Kathi Lutton in particular. Kathi is not only a leading intellectual property partner at Fish & Richardson; she moves mountains. These acknowledgments don't do it justice, but here it goes. Kellyanne Conway of the Polling Company, Saurabh Gupta of Wonder Workshop, David Crawley of Vorto Consulting and Robotics Hacker Dojo, Mallun Yen and Lilly Loh of RPX,

Eric Dezenhall of Dezenhall Resources, Amy Jones of Nordstrom, Christian Josi, Wendy Keller of Keller Media, Francine Parham, Rich Karlgaard of Forbes, Karen Tucker of the Churchill Club, Dana Rubin, Dennis Snow, Chris Stedman of Silicon Valley Bank, Nadia Shouraboura formerly of Amazon and now Hointer, Miguel Castillas of Silicon Valley Links, Roy Chesnutt of Verizon, Art David of Turner Broadcast, Julie Silard Kantor of STEM Connectors, Glenn Dirks of Better Workplace, John Natale of IBM, Luke Hohmann of Conteneo, Norm Happ and Wendy Castleman of Intuit, Johann Jungworth of Mercedes Benz, Patrice Radden and Kimberly Ryan from Red Bull, and Michelle Craig from Intellectual Ventures.

To Robin Murdoch of Accenture who I spent so much time with talking about the new ways of the world and Julie Rosendahl, also of Accenture, who facilitated so much energizing support. To Eric Kutcher, Alex Kazaks, and Michael Uhl of McKinsey & Co. who encouraged me to look at the value of the Silicon Valley mindset as a portable learning and new line of business.

To my editor, Emily Carleton—thank you for tolerating all of my edits, early and late. To Lauren Janiec, Lauren LoPinto, Michelle Fitzgerald, Alan Bradshaw, and the entire Palgrave Macmillan Trade team, including Karen Wolny—thank you for this amazing opportunity to write a second book with you.

To my literary agent, Claudia Cross. It is hard to believe that we have worked together for nearly two decades. Thank you for being so patient with all my ideas and the crazy directions I wish to take my writing.

To my right arm, Jamie Danno, "Where do I begin?" It is not only that you do the work of a dozen people, it is the way you do it—with determination and gusto. Nothing is too daunting for you. In the years we have been working together, I have never heard you use the words, "I can't." You are a unique individual, and I hope you will lean on me to help you go on whatever path you desire.

To my father who inspired my curiosity and love for science.

To my mother, I love you dearly and could not imagine not hearing your voice most every day. To our Harley-loving boy, Mitch, we are blessed you walked into our—now your—family.

To my husband who I continue to laugh with, and I realize after all these years is quite bold as an Ironman—you inspire us as a family. To our three extraordinary children who we share a love for that neither one of us could earlier comprehend. To these children who make us better people: Dominick, to whom I say, "Embrace your unique differences . . . this is the common trait I find of the world's greatest innovators." Drake, "Maintain that eye of the tiger, and the world will be your oyster—with happy fish." To Dayne Alexandria, our "It" girl, "Where nothing scares you, your love and the beautiful way you see the world should be bottled. Keep rocking it."

Notes

INTRODUCTION

1. Tesla Motors, "Hyperloop Alpha." Accessed February 20, 2014, http://www.teslamotors.com/sites/default/files/blog_attachments/hyperloop_alpha3.pdf.
2. Jim Wilson, "Yuri Gagarin: First Man in Space," NASA. Last modified April 13, 2011. Accessed April 22, 2014, http://www.nasa.gov/mission_pages/shuttle/sts1/gagarin_anniversary.html.
3. Email exchange between author and Kellyanne Conway, February 12, 2014.

WHY RISK-TAKING ISN'T GAMBLING

1. Players are dealt two face-down cards. Afterward, each player gets a chance to exercise his betting options. Next, three cards are dealt simultaneously on the table for all players to share. This is called the flop, and it is followed by another round of betting. A fourth card, called the turn, is then dealt, and it too is followed by a round of betting. One final community card called the river is dealt, followed by a final round of betting. When all bets have concluded, there is a showdown, in which the highest-ranking hand in play wins the pot. "How to Play Texas Holdem," The World Series of Poker. Accessed May 12, 2014, http://www.wsop.com/poker-games/texas-holdem/.
2. David Epstein, *The Sports Gene* (New York: Penguin, 2013), 10–14.
3. Michael Gold, "About Jazz Impact." Accessed May 12, 2014, http://www.jazz-impact.com/about.
4. Toyota Company, "Just in Time—Philosophy of Complete Elimination of Waste." Accessed May 21, 2014, http://www.toyota-global.com/company/vision_philosophy/toyota_production_system/just-in-time.html.
5. "Making Operational Innovation Work," *Harvard Management Update* 10, no. 4 (April 2005). Accessed May 12, 2014, http://hbr.org/product/making-operational-innovation-work/an/P0510C-PDF-ENG.
6. Jeffrey Pfeffer and Robert Sutton, *The Knowing-Doing Gap: How Smart Companies Turn Knowledge into Action* (Boston: Harvard Business School Press, 2000).
7. "Making Operational Innovation Work."

8. Quoted in Jane Lee, "Big Achievers Share the Greatest Risks They Ever Took," *Forbes,* March 7, 2011. Accessed April 22, 2014, http://www.forbes.com/2011/03/07/greatest-risk-they-ever-took-2011-entrepreneurs.html.

THE DNA OF A BOLD RISK-TAKER

1. Dina Gachman, "Wingsuit Flyer Jokke Sommer Breaks Down His Epic New Sport," *Redbull U.S.A,* January 30, 2013. Accessed April 22, 2014, http://www.redbullusa.com/cs/Satellite/en_US/Article/Wingsuit-flyer-Jokke-Sommer,-Dream-Lines-IV,-and-interview-021243311413211.
2. Dream Lines IV, "Jokke Sommer on the Sport of Wingsuit Flying 2012," *YouTube* video, 16.25, January 25, 2013. Accessed May 6, 2014, http://www.youtube.com/watch?v=GASFa7rkLtM#t=84.
3. Dr. Lester Keller, "Birdmen: The Original Dream of Flight," *The Atlantic,* March 15, 2012. Accessed May 6, 2014, http://www.theatlantic.com/video/archive/2012/03/a-breathtaking-new-film-about-the-dream-of-human-flight/254430/.
4. Mara Mather and Nicole R. Lighthall, "Risk and Reward Are Processed Differently in Decisions Made under Stress," *Current Directions in Psychological Science* 21, no. 1 (February 2012): 36–41. Accessed April 16, 2014, doi: 10.1177/0963721411429452.
5. Sheryl Ball, Catherine C. Eckel, and Maria Heracleous, "Risk Aversion and Physical Prowess: Prediction, Choice and Bias," *Journal of Risk and Uncertainty* 41, no. 3 (2010): 167–193. Accessed April 16, 2014, doi: 10.1007/s11166-010-9105-x.
6. Ibid.
7. The discussion and quotations in this paragraph are from Thomas Dohmen, Armin Falk, David Huffman, Uwe Sunde, Jurgen Schupp, and Gert G. Wagner, "Individual Risk Attitudes: New Evidence from a Large, Representative, Experimentally-Validated Survey," discussion paper no. 1730 (September 2005). Accessed April 3, 2014, ftp://ftp.iza.org/dps/dp1730.pdf.
8. Alice Park, "Why We Take Risks—It's the Dopamine," *Time,* December 30, 2008. Accessed April 16, 2014, http://content.time.com/time/health/article/0,8599,1869106,00.html.
9. Quoted in Peter Gwin, "The Mystery of Risk," *National Geographic* (June 2013). Accessed April 16, 2014, http://ngm.nationalgeographic.com/2013/06/125-risk-takers/gwin-text.
10. Quoted in Park, "Why We Take Risks."
11. Chris Dillow, "Why Do Some People Take More Risk Than Others?" ING eZonomics (September 2011). Accessed April 5, 2014, http://www.ezonomics.com/blogs/why_do_some_people_take_more_risk_than_others.
12. Adam Smith, "High Testosterone Means High Profits," *Time,* April 14, 2008. Accessed April 3, 2014, http://content.time.com/time/health/article/0,8599,1730662,00.html.
13. Ibid.
14. Daniel Gilbert, *Stumbling on Happiness* (New York: Random House, 2005).

15. Nate Kornell, "Everybody Is Stupid Except You," *Psychology Today*, August 3, 2012. Accessed April 3, 2014, http://www.psychologytoday.com/blog/everybody-is-stupid-except-you/201208/love-win-or-hate-lose.

16. Heidi Grant Halvorson and E. Tory Higgins, "Do You Play to Win—or to Not Lose?" *Harvard Business Review* (March 2013). Accessed April 3, 2014, http://hbr.org/2013/03/do-you-play-to-win-or-to-not-lose/ar/1.

BOLD CHARACTER LEADERSHIP

1. Academy of Achievement, "Jeff Bezos Biography—Academy of Achievement." Last modified November 23, 2013. Accessed May 3, 2014, http://www.achievement.org/autodoc/page/bez0int-1.

2. Bernard Ryan, *Jeff Bezos: Business Executive and Founder of Amazon.com* (New York: Ferguson, 2005), 31.

3. Henry Blodget, "Amazon's Letter to Shareholders Should Inspire Every Company in America," *Business Insider,* April 14, 2013. Accessed May 14, 2014, http://www.businessinsider.com/amazons-letter-to-shareholders-2013-4.

4. Ibid.

5. Quoted in Eric Reguly, "Time to Put an End to the Cult of Shareholder Value," *Globe and Mail,* September 27, 2013. Accessed May 15, 2014, http://www.theglobeandmail.com/report-on-business/rob-magazine/maybe-its-time-for-ceos-to-put-shareholders-second/article14507016/.

6. Michael Jarrett, "CEOs Should Get Out of the Saddle Before They're Pushed Out," *Harvard Business Review* (November 27, 2013). Accessed April 20, 2014, http://blogs.hbr.org/2013/11/ceos-should-get-out-of-the-saddle-before-theyre-pushed-out/.

7. Quoted in Jennifer Liberto, "CEOs Earn 354 Times More than Average Worker," *CNN Money,* April 15, 2013. Accessed April 23, 2014, http://money.cnn.com/2013/04/15/news/economy/ceo-pay-worker/.

8. Quoted in Reguly, "Time to Put an End to the Cult of Shareholder Value."

9. Warren Bennis, *On Becoming a Leader* (Philadelphia, PA: Perseus Books, 1989), 42.

10. Lynda Applegate, Robert Austin, and Elizabeth Collins, "IBM's Decade of Transformation: Turnaround to Growth," *Harvard Business School,* July 8, 2009. Accessed April 22, 2014, http://faculty.washington.edu/socha/css572winter2012/HBR%20IBM%20Decade%20of%20Transformation.pdf.

11. Lisa DiCarlo, "How Lou Gerstner Got IBM to Dance," November 11, 2002. Accessed April 17, 2014, http://www.forbes.com/2002/11/11/cx_ld_1112gerstner.html.

12. R. Austin and R. Nolan, "IBM Corporation: Turnaround 1991–1995," *Harvard Business School,* Case No. 600-098, November 14, 2000, 9. Accessed July 8, 2014, http://teaching.up.edu/bus544/IBM%20turnaround,%202000.pdf.

13. Martha Lagace, "Gerstner: Changing Culture at IBM—Lou Gerstner Discusses Changing the Culture at IBM," December 9, 2002. Accessed July 8, 2014, http://hbswk.hbs.edu/archive/3209.html.

14. Mark Cuban interview, *Piers Morgan Live,* CNN, February 25, 2014.

15. Richard Branson, "The Importance of Mentoring," Virgin. Accessed February 14, 2014, http://www.virgin.com/richard-branson/the-importance-of-mentoring.
16. IBM: IBM press release, "New IBM SyNAPSE Chip Could Open Era of Vast Neural Networks," August 7, 2014. Accessed September 29, 2014, http://www-03.ibm.com/press/us/en/pressrelease/44529.wss. Kurzweil: "The Singularity Is Near," Singularity. Accessed July 8, 2014, http://www.singularity.com.
17. Interview between James Manyika and Andrew McAfee, "Why Every Leader Should Care about Digitization and Disruptive Innovation," McKinsey & Company, January 2014. Accessed April 23, 2014, http://www.mckinsey.com/insights/business_technology/why_every_leader_should_care_about_digitization_and_disruptive_innovation.
18. A statement heard by author that was publicly made by Susan Wojcicki at the "State of Silicon Valley" event in 2013.
19. Author interview with Val Bercovici, November 1, 2013.
20. Elizabeth Buie, "Creative Thinkers Wither with Age," TES, March 25, 2005. Accessed April 14, 2014, http://www.tes.co.uk/article.aspx?storycode=2084549.
21. Author interview with David Crawley, January 19, 2014.
22. Computer History Museum and KQED, "An Evening with Marissa Mayer and NPR's Laura Sydell," *Revolutionaries,* December 18, 2012. Accessed April 23, 2014, https://www.youtube.com/watch?v=FjIdNYr4FtE.
23. Ibid.
24. Marc Benioff, "Share the Model," Salesforce Foundation. Accessed April 1, 2014, http://intl.salesforcefoundation.org/sharethemodel.
25. Marc Benioff acceptance speech, Churchill Club Awards Dinner, September 26, 2013.
26. Ibid.

THE CORPORATE CULTURE OF HOW

1. IDC press release, "Worldwide Integrated Infrastructure and Platforms Revenue Increases 38.5% Year Over Year in the First Quarter of 2014, Surpassing $1.9 Billion in Value, According to IDC," June 26, 2014. Accessed July 13, 2014, http://www.idc.com/getdoc.jsp?containerId=prUS24963914.
2. Author interview with Annalisa Camarillo, October 2013–March 2014, at NetApp's corporate offices in Sunnyvale, CA.
3. NetApp, "Company—Great Place to Work." Accessed May 17, 2014, http://www.netapp.com/us/company/our-story/great-place-to-work/.
4. Ibid.
5. NetApp website, "Best Workplaces." Accessed July 8, 2014, http://www.greatplacetowork.net/best-companies/worlds-best-multinationals/profiles-of-the-winners/1524-3-netapp.
6. Author interview with Tom Georgens, February 14, 2014.
7. Author interviews with Annalisa Camarillo, October 2013–March 2014, at NetApp's corporate office in Sunnyvale, CA.
8. Darrell Rigby and Barbara Bilodeau, "Management Tools and Trends 2007," Bain & Company. Accessed May 17, 2014, http://www.bain.com/management_tools/Management_Tools_and_Trends_2007.pdf; Paul Rogers, Paul Meehan, Scott Tanner, "Building a Winning Culture,"

2006, Bain & Company. Accessed May 17, 2014, http://www.bain.com /Images/BB_Building_winning_culture.pdf; Paul Rogers, "Executives Are Taking a Hard Look at Soft Issues, According to Global Management Study by Bain & Company," Bain & Company press release, March 27, 2007. Accessed October 1, 2014, http://www.bain.com/about/press/press -releases/executives-are-taking-a-hard-look-at-soft-issues.aspx).

9. Quoted in Max Nisen, "HUBSPOT CEO: 99% of Corporate Cultures Are Stuck in the Past," *Business Insider,* June 17, 2013. Accessed February 5, 2014, http://www.businessinsider.com/hubspot-ceo-brian-halligan -on-company-culture-2013-6.

10. Larry Page and Sergey Brin, "2004 Founders' IPO Letter." Accessed April 23, 2014, http://investor.google.com/corporate/2004/ipo-founders-letter .html.

11. Lazlo Bock, "Passion, Not Perks," *Google Think Insights,* September 2011. Accessed May 17, 2014, http://www.thinkwithgoogle.com/articles /passion-not-perks.html.

12. Google website, "Our Culture," accessed October 1, 2014, http://www .google.com/about/company/facts/culture/.

13. Craigslist, "Mission and History." Accessed May 13, 2014, http://www .craigslist.org/about/mission_and_history.

14. Lisa DiCarlo, "How Lou Gerstner Got IBM to Dance," *Forbes,* November 11, 2002. Accessed May 17, 2014, http://www.forbes.com/2002/11/11/cx _ld_1112gerstner.html.

15. Naomi Stanford, *Corporate Culture: Getting It Right* (Hoboken, NJ: John Wiley & Sons, 2011), 161.

16. Danielle Sacks, "Most Innovative Companies 2012," *Fast Company,* February 7, 2012. Accessed May 17, 2014, http://www.fastcompany .com/3017469/most-innovative-companies-2012/34chipotle.

17. Ibid.

18. Elizabeth Olson, "An Animated Ad with a Plot Line and a Moral," *New York Times,* February 9, 2012. Accessed May 17, 2014, www.nytimes .com/2012/02/10/business/media/chipotle-ad-promotes-sustainable-farm ing.html.

THE DEATH OF HR AND THE BIRTH OF TALENTED PEOPLE

1. Author interview with David Rudman, December 11, 2013. All quotes from Rudman are from this source.

2. IDEO, "Life at IDEO." Accessed January 29, 2014, http://www.ideo.com /life-at-ideo.

3. Entrepreneur.com, "Human Resources." Accessed April 22, 2014, http:// www.entrepreneur.com/encyclopedia/human-resources.

4. Quoted in Ekaterina Walter, "Lessons about Building a Team from Zuckerberg," *Entrepreneur,* January 7, 2013. Accessed April 22, 2014, http:// www.entrepreneur.com/article/225369.

5. Edward Lawler, "Human Resources: It's Time for a Reset," *Forbes,* November 20, 2011. Accessed April 22, 2014, http://www.forbes.com/sites /edwardlawler/2011/11/30/human-resources-its-time-for-a-reset/.

6. Aparna Sharma, "Why Choose a Career in Human Resources?" *Times Jobs,* December 3, 2013. Accessed April 22, 2014, http://content.times jobs.com/why-choose-a-career-in-human-resources/.

7. Sources: Baby Boomers: History.com, "Baby Boomers." Accessed July 22, 2014, http://www.history.com/topics/baby-boomers; Lynn G. Gre, *The Rise and Fall of American Technology* (New York: Algora, 2010), 38; Steve Greenburg, "Transistor Radios: The Technology That Ignited Beatlemania," CBS News, February 1, 2014. Accessed July 21, 2014, http://www.cbsnews.com/news/transistor-radios-the-technology-that-ignited-beatlemania/.

    Generation X: Jessica R. Sincavage, "The Labor Force and Unemployment: Three Generations of Change," Bureau of Labor Statistics (June 2004). Accessed July 21, 2014, http://www.bls.gov/opub/mlr/2004/06/art2full.pdf.

    Millennials: Kathryn Zickuhr, "Generations 2010," Pew Research Internet Project, December 16, 2010. Accessed July 22, 2014, http://www.pewinternet.org/2010/12/16/generations-2010/; US Chamber of Commerce Foundation, "The Millennial Generation Research Review," research conducted 2009 to 2012. Accessed July 21, 2014, http://www.uschamberfoundation.org/millennial-generation-research-review; Adam Lella and Andrew Lipsman, "Marketing to Millennials: 5 Things Every Marketer Should Know," comScore White Paper, February 14, 2014. Accessed July 21, 2014, https://www.comscore.com/Insights/Presentations-and-Whitepapers/2014/Marketing-to-Millennials-5-Things-Every-Marketer-Should-Know; Ian Shapira, "Texting Generation Doesn't Share Boomers' Taste for Talk," *Washington Post*, August 8, 2010. Accessed July 22, 2014, http://www.washingtonpost.com/wp-dyn/content/article/2010/08/07/AR2010080702848.html.

8. Nicholas Donofrio, Jim Spohrer, and Hossein S. Zadeh, "Research-Driven Medical Education and Practice: A Case for T-Shaped Professionals," *Viewpoint MJA,* Michigan State University Research. Accessed May 21, 2014, http://www.ceri.msu.edu/wp-content/uploads/2010/06/A-Case-for-T-Shaped-Professionals-20090907-Hossein.pdf.

9. Sharma, "Why Choose a Career in Human Resources?"

10. Phone interview between author and Francine Parham, April 18, 2014.

11. U.S. Bureau of Labor Statistics, "Employee Tenure in 2012." Last modified September 18, 2012. Accessed April 22, 2014, http://www.bls.gov/news.release/pdf/tenure.pdf.

12. Susan Heathfield, "Keep Your Best: Retention Tips," About.com Human Resources. Accessed May 21, 2014, http://humanresources.about.com/cs/retention/a/turnover.htm.

13. Quoted in Farhad Manjoo, "The Happiness Machine," *Slate,* January 21, 2013. Accessed April 22, 2014, http://www.slate.com/articles/technology/technology/2013/01/google_people_operations_the_secrets_of_the_world_s_most_scientific_human.html.

14. SHRM, "SHRM Workplace Forecast." Last modified 2013. Accessed February 12, 2014, http://www.shrm.org/research/futureworkplacetrends/documents/13-0146%20workplace_forecast_full_fnl.pdf.

15. Author interview with Julie Silard Kantor, October 22, 2014.

16. U.S. Bureau of Labor Statistics, "Employment Projections." Accessed March 28, 2014, http://www.bls.gov/emp/.

17. "What's Driving Dropout Rate for Black, Latino Men?," NPR, September 20, 2012. Accessed May 21, 2014, http://www.npr.org/2012/09/20/161475627/whats-driving-dropout-rate-for-black-latino-men.

18. Susan Lund, James Manyika, Scott Nyquist, Lenny Mendonca, and Sreenivas Ramaswamy, "Game Changers: Five Opportunities for US Growth and Renewal," McKinsey & Co., July 2013. Accessed April 22, 2014, http://www.mckinsey.com/insights/americas/us_game_changers.

19. STEMconnector, "100 CEO Leaders in STEM," 13, 47. Accessed October 29, 2013, http://www.stemconnector.org/sites/default/files/100-CEO-Leaders-in-STEM-web.pdf.

20. Ibid., 213.

21. Tata Consultancy Services press release, "TCS' goIT Student Technology Program Encourages Students to Pursue STEM Fields in Columbus, Ohio," July 10, 2013. Accessed May 21, 2014, http://www.tcs.com/news_events/press_releases/Pages/TCS-goIT-Student-Technology-Program-STEM-Columbus.aspx

22. All quotes from Jemison are from an email interview between Jamie Danno, *The Risk Factor* research assistant, and Tom Jemison, February 16, 2014.

IMPROVISATIONAL INNOVATION

1. Author interview with Tom Georgens at NetApp, March 5, 2014.

2. Cirque Du Soleil, "About Us." Accessed April 21, 2014, http://www.cirq uedusoleil.com/en/home/about-us/at-a-glance.aspx.

3. Clay Christensen, "Key Concepts: Disruptive Innovation." Accessed April 21, 2014, http://www.claytonchristensen.com/key-concepts/.

4. Author interviews with Dave Blakely, August 2013–March 2014.

5. D.school learning experiences, "Attend Executive Education: Success Stories." Accessed July 30, 2014, http://dschool.stanford.edu/learning-expe riences/.

6. Ibid.

7. University of California, Berkeley, Haas School of Business, "Program in Open Innovation." Accessed April 21, 2014, http://openinnovation .berkeley.edu/what_is_oi.html.

8. Author interviews with Blakely.

9. Author interview with Paul Jacobs, San Diego, February 18, 2014.

10. Gary Hamel, *The Future of Management* (Boston, MA: Harvard Business School, 2007).

11. Email exchange between Jamie Danno, *The Risk Factor* research assistant, and Qualcomm marketing manager, April 30, 2014.

12. Computer History Museum, "The Homebrew Computer Club." Accessed March 17, 2014, http://www.computerhistory.org/revolution/personal -computers/17/312.

13. Hacker Dojo, "About." Accessed April 21, 2014, http://www.hackerdojo .com/About.

14. Author interview with David Crawley, January 19, 2014.

15. Ibid.

INTELLECTUAL PROPERTY

1. Kathi Lutton interview with Richard Lutton, April 12, 2014.

2. Ibid.

3. Felix Richter, "IBM Tops U.S. Patent Ranking for 21st Consecutive Year," *Statista,* January 17, 2014. Accessed April 10, 2014, http://www.statista .com/chart/1796/us-patent-ranking-2013.

4. Kathi Lutton interview with Jim Malackowski, April 20, 2014.

5. Carol A. Corrado and Charles R. Hulten, "How Do You Measure a 'Technological Revolution'?," January 05, 2007, accessed October 1, 2014, https://www.aeaweb.org/aer/data/may2010/aer_100_2_99_app.pdf.

6. Fritz Machlup and Edith Penrose, "The Patent Controversy in the Nineteenth Century," *Journal of Economic History* 10, no. 1 (1950): 1–29. http://c4sif.org/wp-content/uploads/2010/09/Machlup-Penrose-The-Pat ent-Controversy-in-the-Nineteenth-Century-1950-b.pdf.

7. Ibid.

8. B. Zorina Khan, "Trolls and Other Patent Inventions: Economic History and the Patent Controversy in the Twenty-first Century," August 2013. Accessed April 23, 2014, http://cpip.gmu.edu/wp-content/uploads/2013/08 /Khan-Zorina-Trolls-and-Other-Patent-Inventions.pdf.

9. Ibid.

10. Author phone interviews with Joseph Schuman, April 16–May 2014.

11. Author in-person and phone interviews with Kathi Lutton, February– May 2014.

12. Nathan Myhrvold, "Funding Eureka!" *Harvard Business Review,* March 2010. Accessed July 10, 2014, http://i2ge.com/wp-content/uploads /2012/01/Funding-Eureka.pdf.

13. Malcolm Gladwell, "In the Air," *The New Yorker,* May 12, 2008. Accessed July 11, 2014, http://www.newyorker.com/reporting/2008/05/12 /080512fa_fact_gladwell?currentPage=all.

14. Michael Orey, "Inside Nathan Myhrvold's Mysterious New Idea Machine," *Bloomberg BusinessWeek,* July 2, 2006. Accessed July 11, 2014, http://www.businessweek.com/stories/2006-07-02/inside-nathan-myhr volds-mysterious-new-idea-machine.

15. Conversations between Kathi Lutton and Nathan Myhrvold, April–May 2014.

16. Conversation between Kathi Lutton and Jim Malackowski, April 30, 2014.

17. U.S. Accounting Principles Board, "APB 17: Intangible Assets." August 1970. Accessed July 11, 2014, http://www.fasb.org/cs/BlobServer?blob key=id&blobnocache=true&blobwhere=1175820195241&blobheader =application/pdf&blobcol=urldata&blobtable=MungoBlobs.

18. "IAS 22—Business Combinations," *International Accounting Standards Plus*. Accessed July 31, 2014, http://www.iasplus.com/en/standards/ias/ias 22.

19. "Financial Reporting Standard—10 Goodwill and Intangible Assets," *The Accounting Standard Board Limited,* December 1997. Accessed August 3, 2014, https://www.frc.org.uk/Our-Work/Publications/ASB /FRS-10-Goodwill-and-Intangible-Assets/FRS-10-Goodwill-and-Intan gible-Assets.aspx, 9-14.

20. "Accounting for Business Combinations, Goodwill and Other Intangible Assets," Financial Accounting Standards Board, preface, xv. Accessed August 3, 2014, http://www.iasplus.com/en/binary/dttpubs/0705applyingfas 141and142.pdf.

21. "IAS 30- Intangible Assets," *International Accounting Standards Plus.* Accessed August 3, 2014, http://www.iasplus.com/en/standards/ias/ias38.
22. "Taxation of Cross-border Mergers and Acquisitions," KPMG, 2010, Accessed August 3, 2014, https://www.kpmg.com/Global/en/IssuesAnd Insights/ArticlesPublications/Lists/Expired/TAX-MA-2010/MA_Cross -Border_2010_Germany.pdf, introduction.
23. Author in-person and phone interviews with Kathi Lutton, February– May 2014.
24. Ibid.
25. Email exchange between author and Stephen LaFalce, senior research librarian, Fish & Richardson, October 1, 2014.
26. Author in-person and phone interviews with Kathi Lutton, February– May 2014.

SMART WORK

1. Camille Ryan and Julie Siebens, "Educational Attainment in the United States: 2009," *U.S. Census Bureau,* February 2012. Accessed April 23, 2014, https://www.census.gov/prod/2012pubs/p20-566.pdf.
2. George Avalos, "Inside Google's Million Square Foot Expansion," *Oakland Tribune,* September 24, 2013. Accessed July 22, 2014, http://www .berkshireeagle.com/business/ci_24163219/inside-googles-million-square -foot-expansion.
3. Paul Goldberger, "Exclusive Preview: Google's New Built-from-Scratch Googleplex," February 22, 2013. Accessed July 20, 2014, http://www .vanityfair.com/online/daily/2013/02/exclusive-preview-googleplex.
4. United States Census Bureau, "Megacommuters: 600,000 in U.S. Travel 90 Minutes and 50 Miles to Work, and 10.8 Million Travel an Hour Each Way, Census Bureau Reports," March 5, 2013. Accessed July 22, 2014, http://www.census.gov/newsroom/releases/archives/american_commu nity_survey_acs/cb13-41.html.
5. Johann "JJ" Jungwirth speech, Churchill Club, Silicon Valley, June 23, 2014.
6. Email exchanges between author and Johann "JJ" Jungwirth, June 30– July 17, 2014.
7. Ibid.
8. Author interview with Glenn Dirks, October 24, 2013.
9. Better Workplace, "WorkFit Introduction." Accessed on October 30, 2013, http://www.betterworkplace.com/workfit_introduction.
10. Kathleen D. Vohs, Joseph P. Redden, and Ryan Rahinel, "Physical Order Produces Healthy Choices, Generosity, and Conventionality, Whereas Disorder Produces Creativity," February 1, 2013. Accessed October 30, 2013, http://pss.sagepub.com/content/24/9/1860.
11. Kenneth Matos and Ellen Galinsky, "National Study of Employers 2012," *Families and Work Institute,* 2012. Accessed November 7, 2013, http:// familiesandwork.org/site/research/reports/NSE_2012.pdf.
12. Thomas Lee, "Best Buy Ends Flexible Work Program for Its Corporate Employees," *Star Tribune,* March 5, 2013. Accessed October 28, 2013, http://www.startribune.com/business/195156871.html?refer=y.
13. Ibid.

14. Max Nisen, "Best Buy Dropping Flexible Work," *Business Insider,* March 5, 2013. Accessed October 28, 2013, http://www.businessinsider.com /best-buy-dropping-flexible-work-2013-3.

15. Cali Ressler, "Welcome to the Past: Best Buy Embraces Last Century Management Practices," *Results-Only Work Environment,* March 5, 2013. Accessed July 31, 2014, http://info.gorowe.com/blog/bid/327538 /Welcome-to-the-Past-Best-Buy-Embraces-Last-Century-Management -Practices.

16. Dana Wilkie, "Despite Research Supporting Flexible Work Schedules, Angst Still Exists," SHRM, October 31, 2013. Accessed March 24, 2014, https://www.shrm.org/hrdisciplines/employeerelations/articles/Pages /Flexible-Work-Schedule-Yahoo-Best-Buy.aspx.

17. Ibid.

18. Ibid.

19. Nicholas Bloom, "To Raise Productivity, Let More Employees Work from Home," *Harvard Business Review* (January–February 2014). Accessed March 24, 2014, http://hbr.org/2014/01/to-raise-productivity-let -more-employees-work-from-home/ar/1.

20. Caroline Humer, "In Telecommuting Debate, Aetna Sticks by Big At-Home Workforce," Reuters, March 1, 2013. Accessed October 28, 2013, http://www.reuters.com/article/2013/03/01/us-yahoo-telecommuting -aetna-idUSBRE92006820130301.

21. All slides are from the Netflix slide deck available at Reed Hastings, "Netflix Culture: Freedom & Responsibility," August 1, 2009. Accessed May 17, 2014, http://www.slideshare.net/reed2001/culture-1798664.

22. Tony Schwartz, "Relax! You'll Be More Productive," *New York Times,* February 9, 2013. Accessed March 24, 2014, http://www.nytimes .com/2013/02/10/opinion/sunday/relax-youll-be-more-productive.html ?pagewanted=1&_r=0.

23. Mark R. Rosekind et al., "The Cost of Poor Sleep: Workplace Productivity Loss and Associated Costs," *Journal of Occupational & Environmental Medicine* 52, no. 1 (2010): 91–98. Accessed May 17, 2014, http:// journals.lww.com/joem/toc/2010/01000.

24. yourSabbatical.com, "Benefits & Types." Accessed March 24, 2014, http://yoursabbatical.com/learn/types-of-sabbaticals/.

25. Cited in Schwartz, "Relax! You'll Be More Productive."

26. Daniel Cook, "What Are Game Mechanics?," Lost Garden, October 23, 2006. Accessed October 2, 2014, http://www.lostgarden.com/2006/10 /what-are-game-mechanics.html.

27. Jesse Schell at DICE 2010, "Design Outside the Box" Presentation, February 18, 2010, video clip. Accessed July 16, 2014, http://www.g4tv.com /videos/44277/dice-2010-design-outside-the-box-presentation/.

DECISION-MAKING AMID THE CLUTTER

1. East West Digital News, "OZON Group Press Release." Last modified March 28, 2013. Accessed April 22, 2014, http://www.ewdn.com /2013/03/28/ozon-group-reached-492-million-gmv-and-250-million-net -sales-in-2012/.

2. Max Chafkin, "Is This the Jeff Bezos of Russia?" *Fast Company,* August 8, 2012. Accessed April 22, 2014, http://www.fastcompany.com/3000043 /jeff-bezos-russia.

3. Morgan Stanley research, "Russian Ecommerce at the Tipping Point," January 6, 2014. Accessed October 17, 2014, http://static.squarespace .com/static/52e0a957e4b0bcc6b2274958/t/52fa9ec9e4b052e52d a9a4a6/1392156361135/Russia_eCommerce_Morgan%20Stanley.pdf, pg. 7.

4. Dan Lovallo and Olivier Sibony, "The Case for Behavioral Strategy" *McKinsey & Co.*, March 2010. Accessed April 22, 2014, http://www .mckinsey.com/insights/strategy/the_case_for_behavioral_strategy.

5. Melinda Merino, "You Can't Be a Wimp—Make the Tough Calls," *Harvard Business Review* (November 2013). Accessed April 22, 2014, http:// hbr.org/2013/11/you-cant-be-a-wimp-make-the-tough-calls/ar/1.

6. Ibid.

7. Interview between Jamie Danno, *The Risk Factor* research assistant, and NetApp employees, February 5, 2014.

8. Ibid., February 4, 2014.

9. Ibid., February 5, 2014.

10. Joel Hersch, "Big Data," *Good Times Weekly,* January 15, 2014. Accessed April 22, 2014, http://www.gtweekly.com/index.php/santa-cruz-news /good-times-cover-stories/5343-big-data.html.

11. Zettaset, "What Is Big Data?" Accessed April 22, 2014, http://www .zettaset.com/info-center/what-is-big-data.

12. Hersch, "Big Data."

13. Ibid.

14. David J. Snowden and Mary E. Boone, "A Leader's Framework for Decision Making," *Harvard Business Review* (November 2007). Accessed April 22, 2014, http://hbr.org/2007/11/a-leaders-framework-for-decision-making/.

15. Interview between Jamie Danno, *The Risk Factor* research assistant, and John Natale, IBM external relations. February 5–24, 2014.

16. IBM press release, "IBM Forms New Watson Group to Meet Growing Demand for Cognitive Innovations," January 9, 2014. Accessed October 1, 2014, https://www-03.ibm.com/press/us/en/pressrelease/42867.wss.

17. Author interview with Nadia Shouraboura, November 8, 2013.

18. James Surowiecki, *The Wisdom of Crowds* (New York: Anchor, 2005), xii–xiii.

19. Ben Lillie, "Of Oxes and the Wisdom of Crowds: Lori Zoref at TED2012," TED blog, February 29, 2012. Accessed March 24, 2014, http://blog .ted.com/2012/02/29/of-oxes-and-the-wisdom-of-crowds-lior-zoref-at -ted2012/

20. Surowiecki, *The Wisdom of Crowds,* xiii–xiv.

21. Author interview and Luke Hohmann, March 6, 2014.

BRANDING AND MARKETING NOISE

1. Kem Symon, Connie Henderson, and Iain Gray, "Branson Down—and Out of Daredevil Life for Good," *Glasgow Herald,* July 4, 1987. Accessed April 20, 2014, http://news.google.com/newspapers?nid=2507&dat=1987 0704&id=Pqw1AAAAIBAJ&sjid=D6YLAAAAIBAJ&pg=3470,880778.

2. Red Bull Stratos. "The Mission." Accessed February 2, 2013, http://www .redbullstratos.com/the-mission/what-is-the-mission/.

3. Ashling O'Connor, "Felix Baumgartner's Plunge from Stratosphere Breaks Broadcast Records," *The Australian,* October 16, 2012. Accessed February 4, 2013, http://www.theaustralian.com.au/news/world

/felix-baumgartners-plunge-from-stratosphere-breaks-broadcast-records
/story-fnb64oi6-1226496913671.

4. Darren Heitner, "Red Bull Stratos Worth Tens of Millions of Dollars in Global Exposure for the Red Bull Brand," *Forbes,* October 15, 2012. Accessed February 20, 2014, http://www.forbes.com/sites/darrenheitner /2012/10/15/red-bull-stratos-worth-tens-of-millions-of-dollars-in-global -exposure-for-the-red-bull-brand/.

5. "CMO Survey Report," The CMO Survey, August 2014. Accessed October 16, 2014, http://cmosurvey.org/files/2014/09/The_CMO_Survey -Highlights_and_Insights-Aug-2014.pdf.

6. Matt Jauchius, "The Evolution of the CMO: More Strategic and Analytical," February 6, 2013. Video clip. Accessed March 15, 2014, http://youtu .be/ifeYS4nKVec.

7. "Less Guff, More Puff," *Economist,* May 18, 2013. Accessed March 18, 2014, http://www.economist.com/news/business/21578063-thanks-new -digital-tools-marketing-no-longer-voodoo-less-guff-more-puff.

8. "Gilt Groupe: Using Big Data, Mobile and Social Media to Reinvent Shopping," McKinsey & Company, November 2012. Accessed March 25, 2014, http://www.mckinsey.com/client_service/marketing_and_sales/latest_ thinking/using_big_data_mobile_and_social_media_to_reinvent_shop ping.

9. Kevin Randall, "It's a Fact: Strong Brands Drive B2B Markets," Movéo Integrated Branding. Accessed May 18, 2014, http://www.moveo.com /data/Articles/EFFECTIVEEXEC_article.pdf.

10. Ibid.

11. Ibid.

12. Author interviews with Annalisa Camarillo, October 2013–March 2014.

13. Ibid.

14. "BrandVoice,"*Forbes Media.* Accessed March 28, 2014, http://www .forbesmedia.com/category/brandvoice/.

THE ERA OF COLLABORATIVE SALES AND CUSTOMER SERVICE

1. Author interview with Norman Happ, February 10, 2014.

2. The text discussion of Design for Delight and quotes from Wendy Castleman are from an interview between the author and the author's research assistant, Jamie Danno, with Wendy Castleman, February 26, 2014.

3. Ibid.

4. Brent Adamson, Matthew Dixon, and Nicholas Toman, "Dismantling the Sales Machine," *Harvard Business Review* (November 2013). Accessed March 28, 2014, http://hbr.org/2013/11/dismantling-the-sales-machine /ar/1.

5. Unless otherwise noted, all quotes from Dennis Snow are from a phone and email exchange between the author and Snow, July 16, 2014.

6. "Cramer's 'Hospitality' Index," May 10, 2012. Accessed July 14, 2014, http://video.cnbc.com/gallery/?video=3000089407. CNBC *Mad Money.*

7. Study cited in Dennis Snow and Teri Yanovitch, *Unleashing Excellence: The Complete Guide to Ultimate Customer Service* (Hoboken, NJ: John Wiley & Sons, 2010), xvi.

8. Brent Adamson, Matthew Dixon, and Nicholas Toman, "Dismantling the Sales Machine," *Harvard Business Review* (November 2013). Accessed

March 28, 2014, http://hbr.org/2013/11/dismantling-the-sales-machine/ar/1.

9. Brent Adamson, Matthew Dixon and Nicholas Toman, "Why Individuals No Longer Rule on Sales Teams," *Harvard Business Review*, January 2014. Accessed March 28, 2014, http://blogs.hbr.org/2014/01/why-the-individual-no-longer-rules-in-sales/.

10. HootSuite Press Release, "HootSuite Empowers Sales and Customer Service Teams with SugarCRM App Integration," August 29, 2013. Accessed April 22, 2014, http://media.hootsuite.com/sugarcrm-app-integration/.

11. Ibid.

12. Christina Rogers, "Say Goodbye to the Car Salesman," *Wall Street Journal,* November 20, 2013. Accessed April 22, 2014, http://online.wsj.com/news/articles/SB10001424052702304672404579182061400578466.

13. Ken DeLeon Realty advertisement, *Daily News* (Palo Alto), February 7, 2013. Accessed February 10, 2013.

14. Email exchange between Jessica Rose, NetApp, and Jamie Danno, *The Risk Factor* research assistant, February 4, 2014.

15. Email exchange between Amy Jones, VP of corporate affairs at Nordstrom, and Jamie Danno, *The Risk Facto*r research assistant, September 12, 2013.

"YES, AND . . . ?"

1. Rob Slitanen "The Real Story behind Apple's 'Think Different' Campaign," *Forbes*, December 14, 2011. Accessed August 1, 2014, http://www.forbes.com/sites/onmarketing/2011/12/14/the-real-story-behind-apples-think-different-campaign/.

Index